Simone Sereni

Wings and Brushes

Bird Lover's Coloring Book

Coloring Book

ISBN: 9798857840511

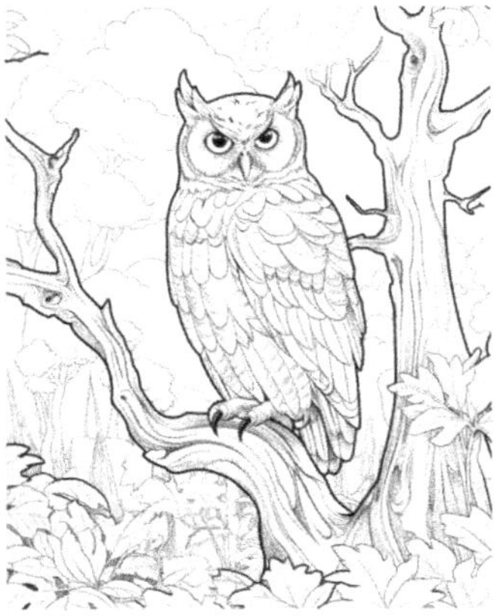
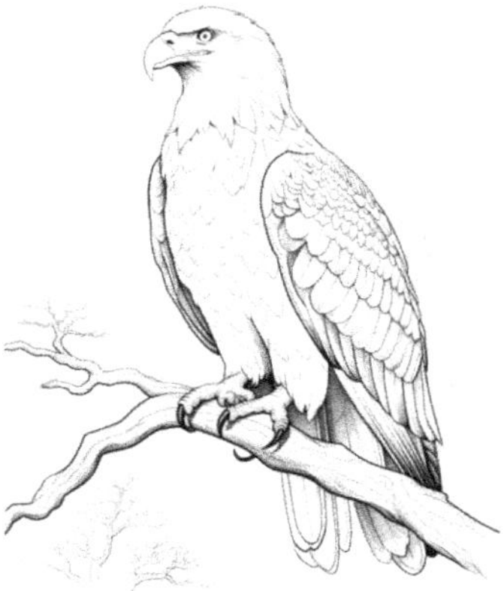
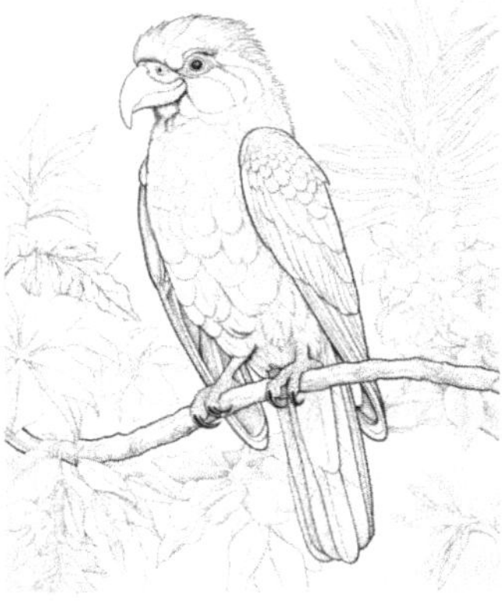
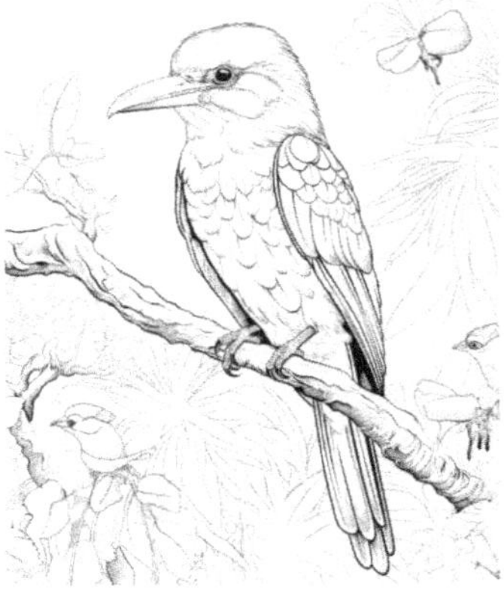
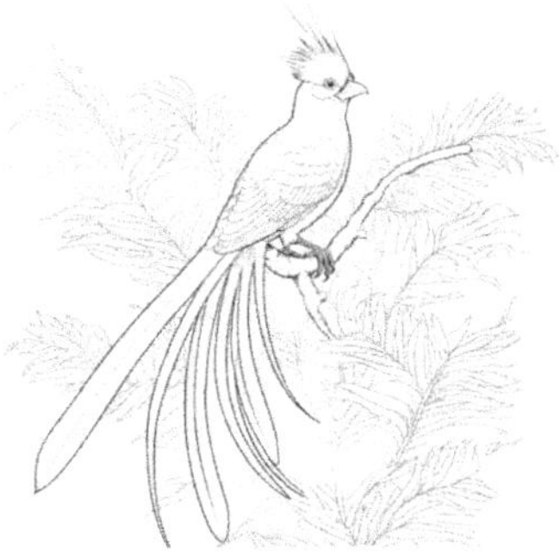
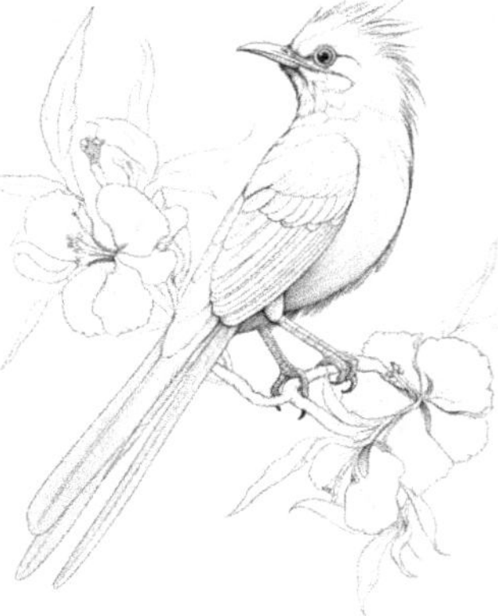
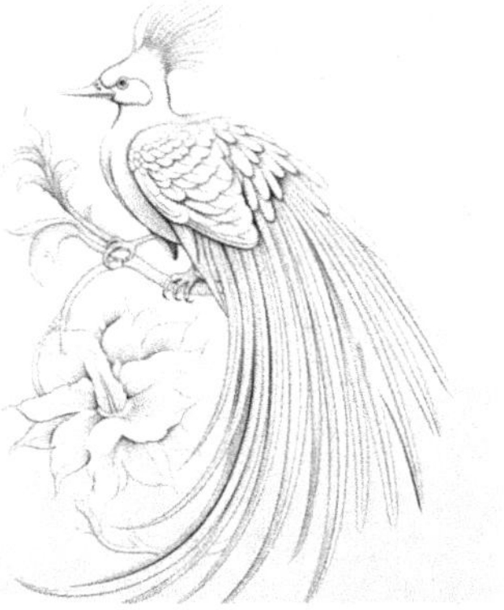
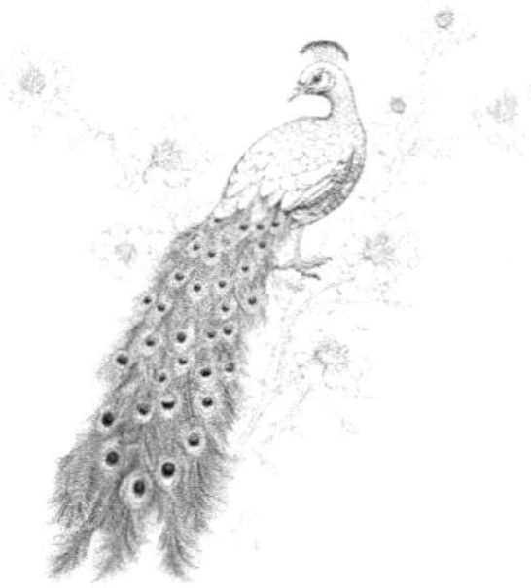
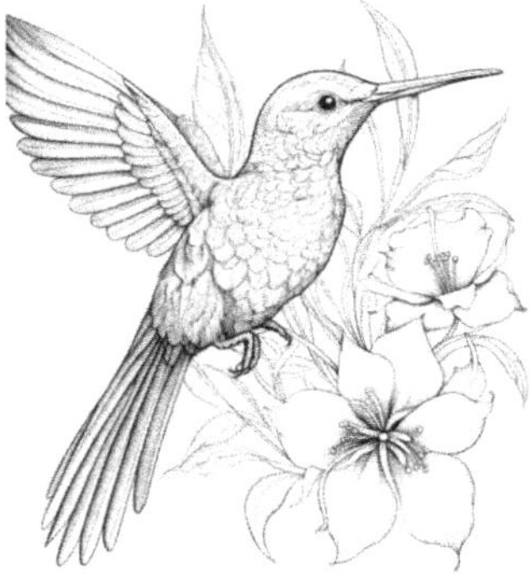
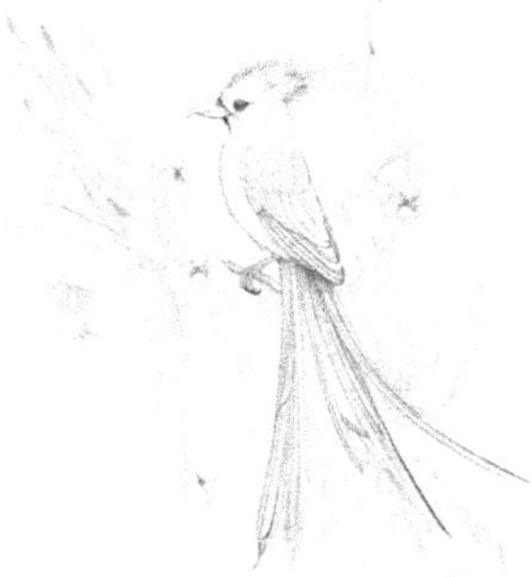
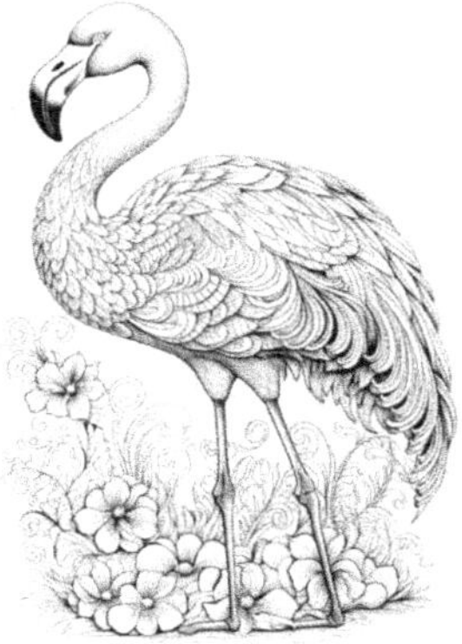
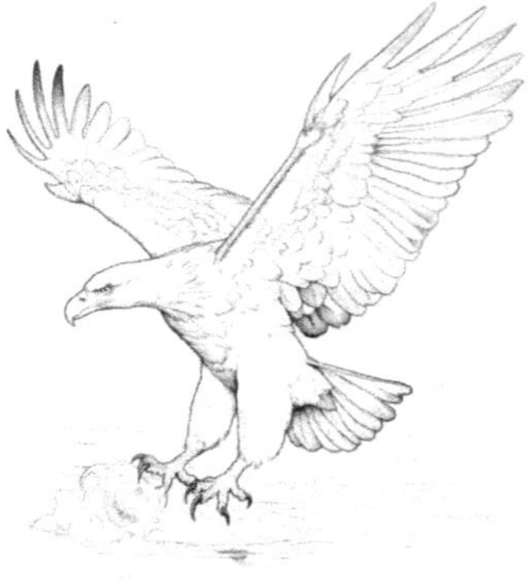
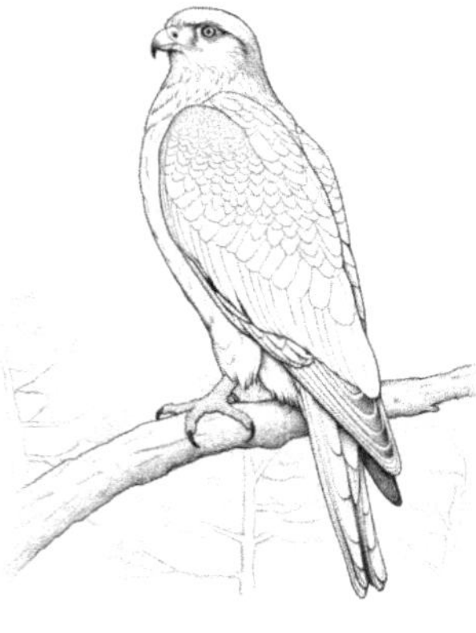
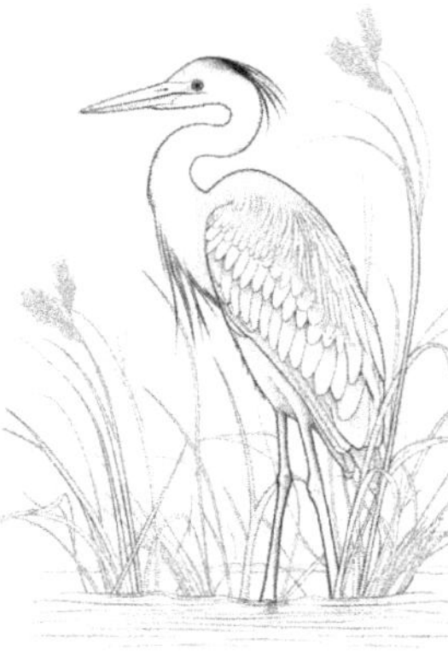
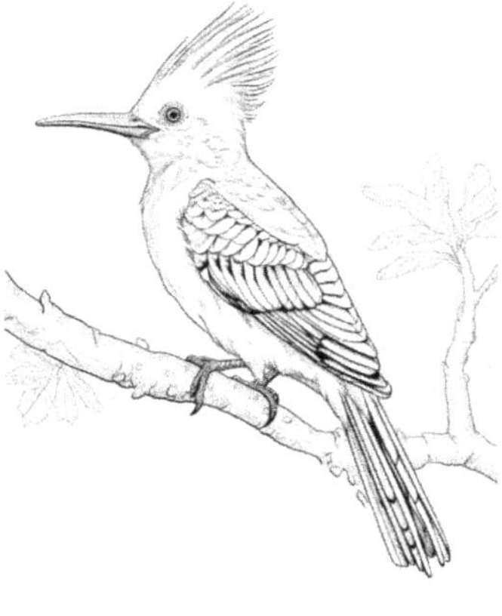

more than 50
coloring images

Color Test Page

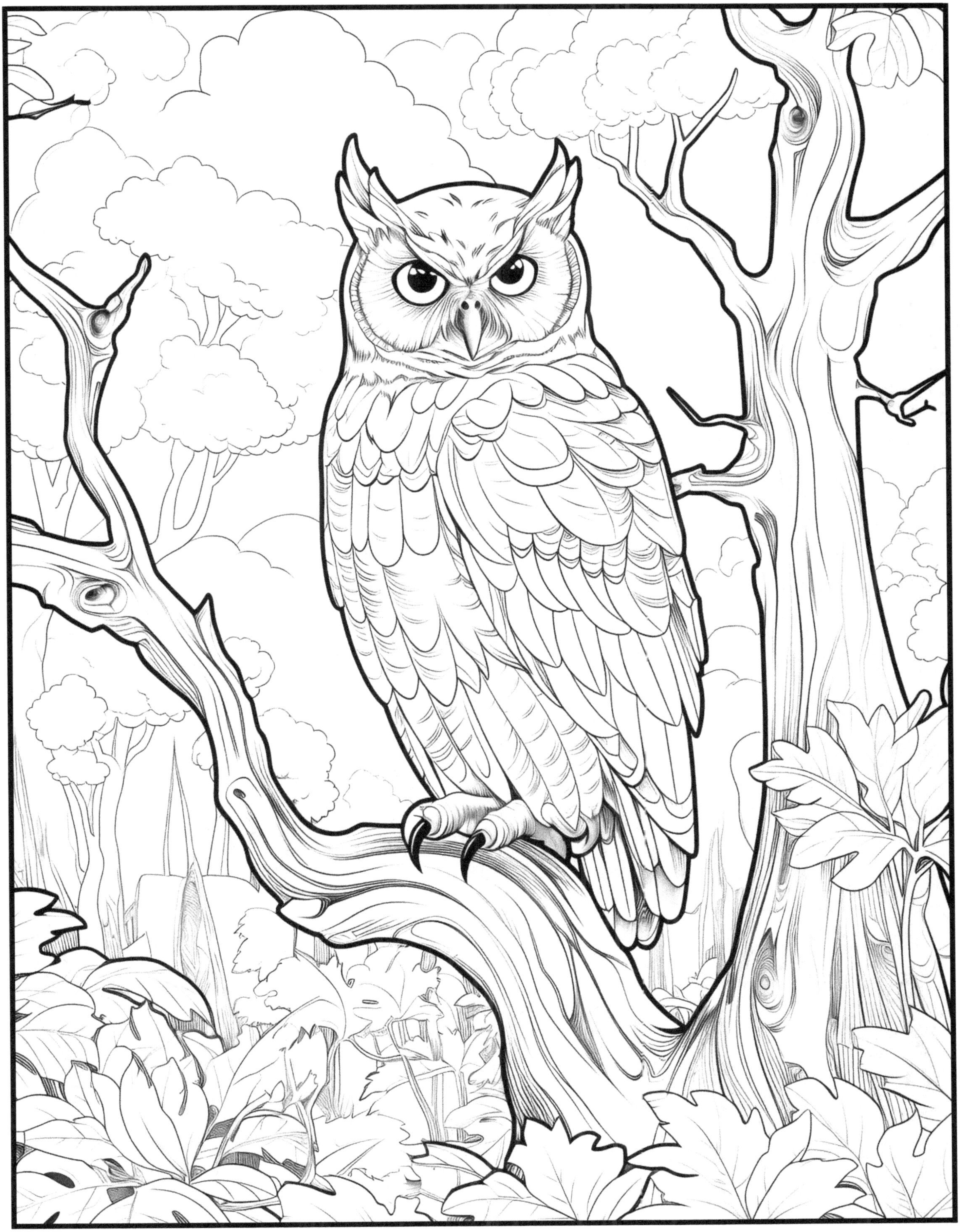

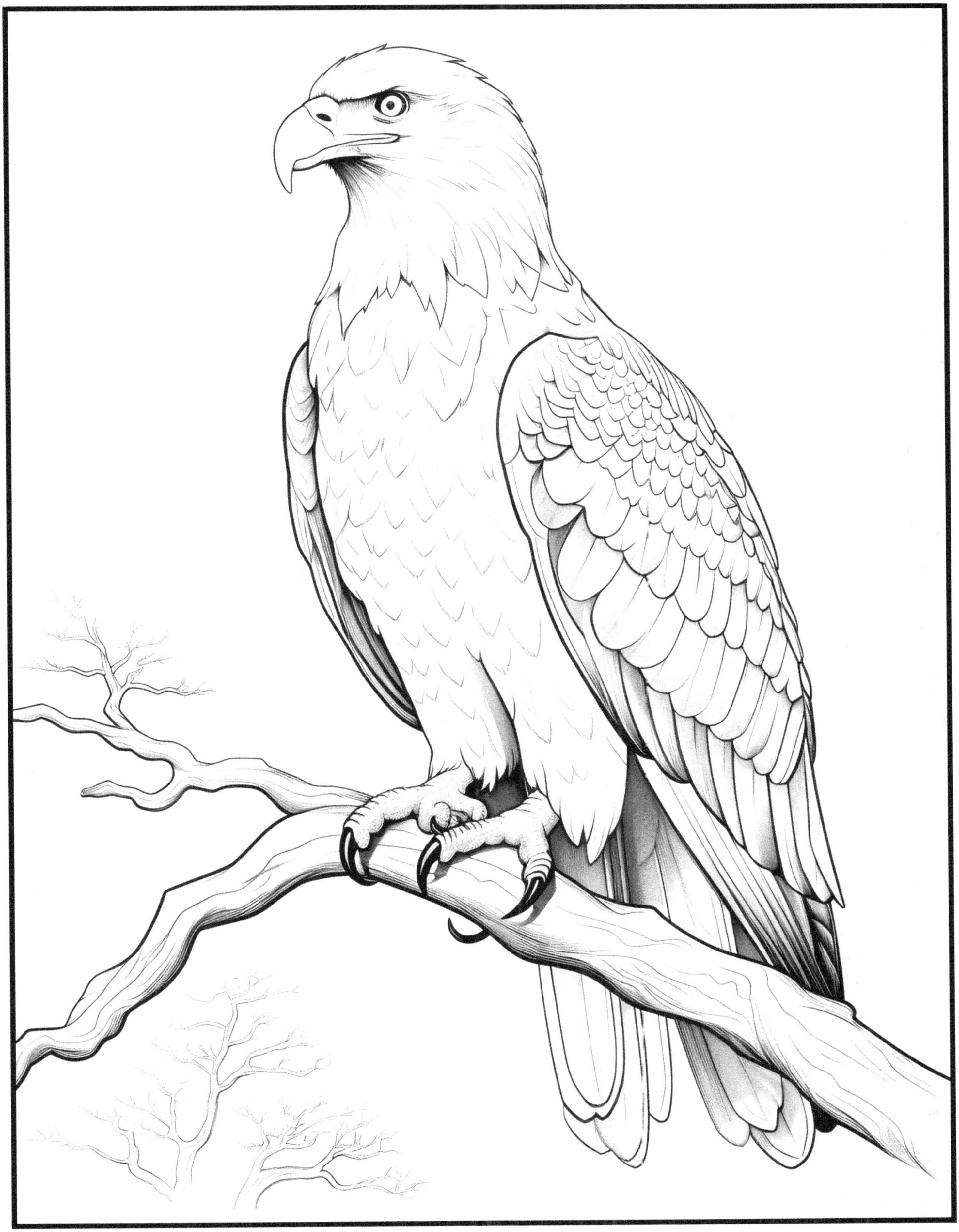

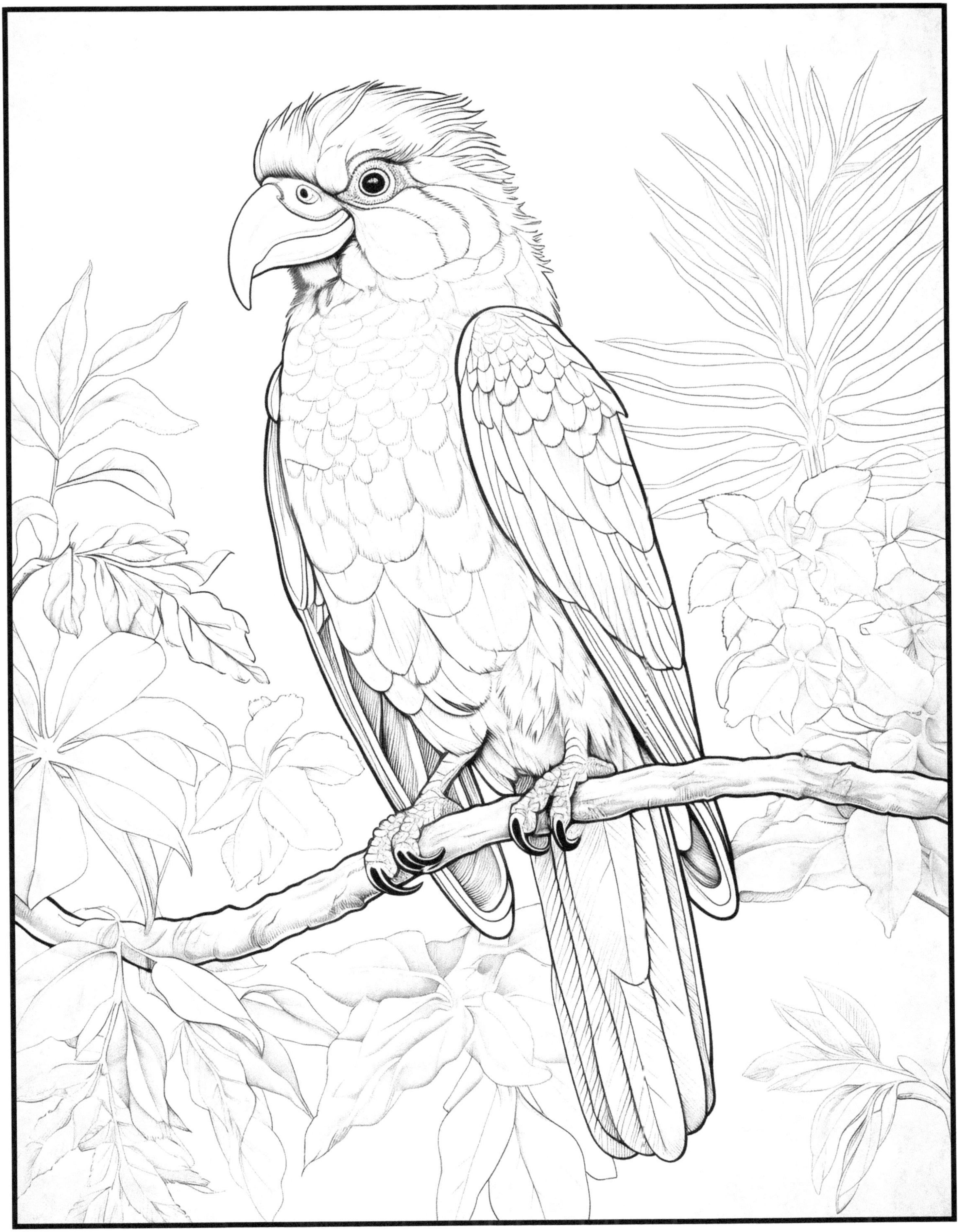

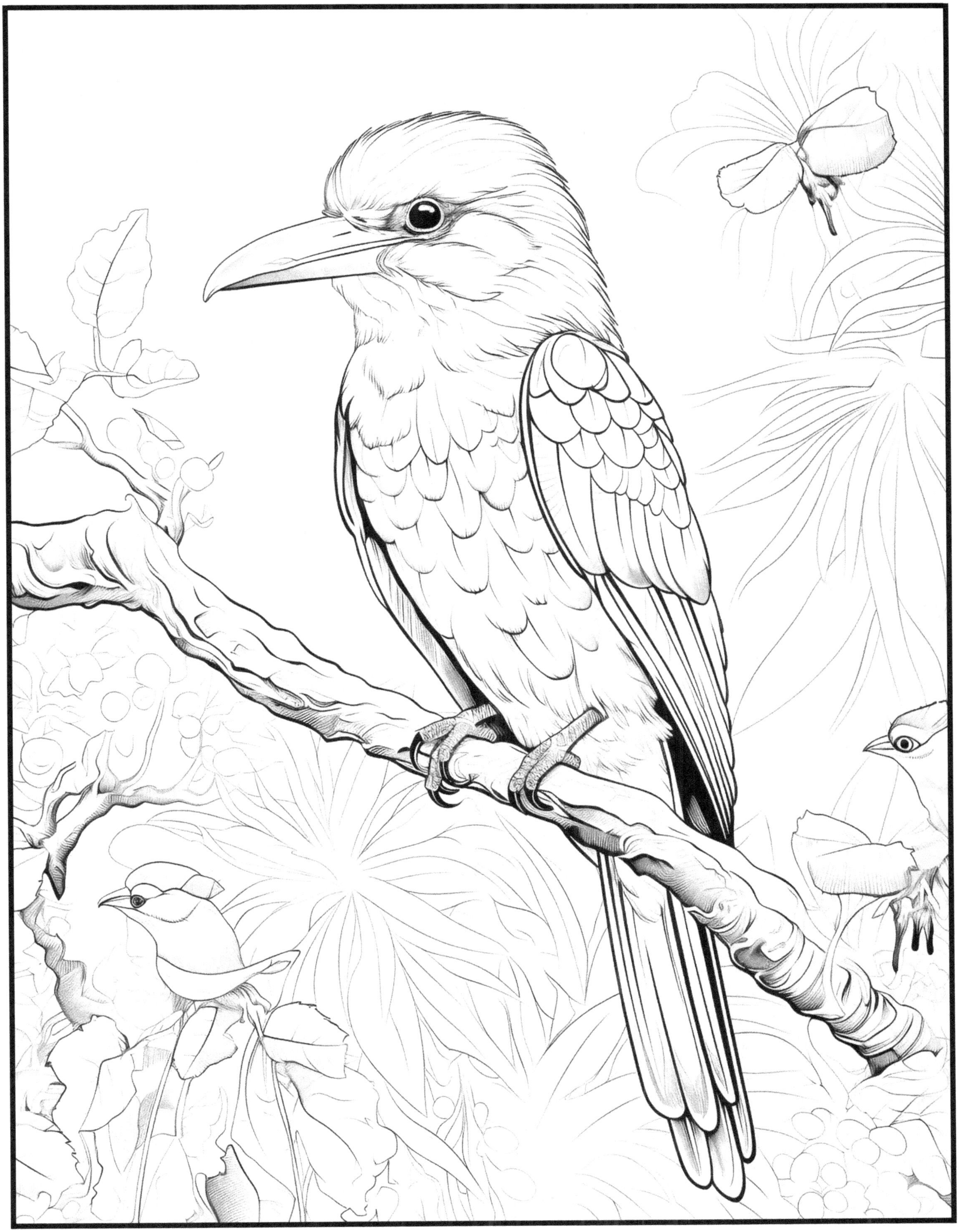

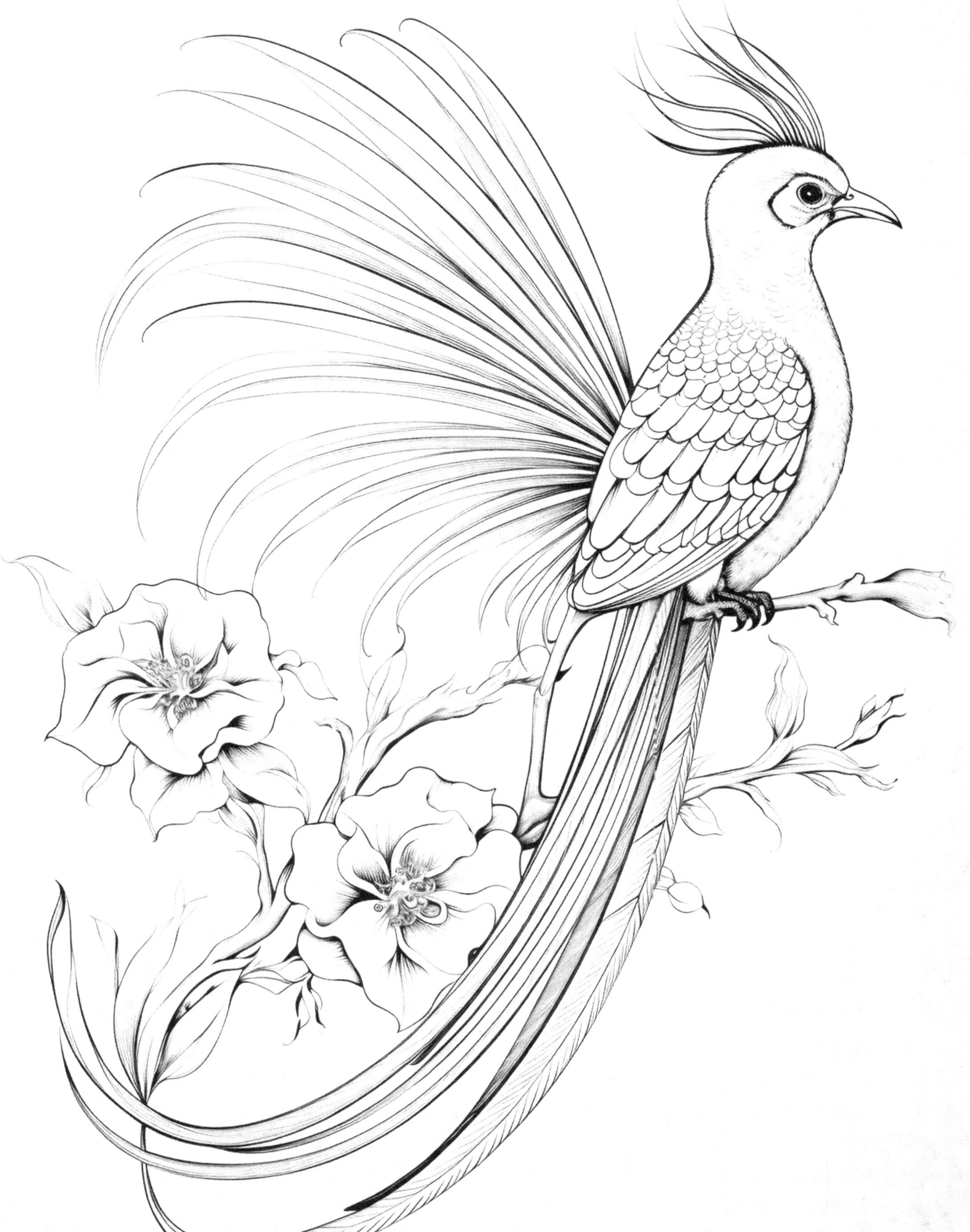

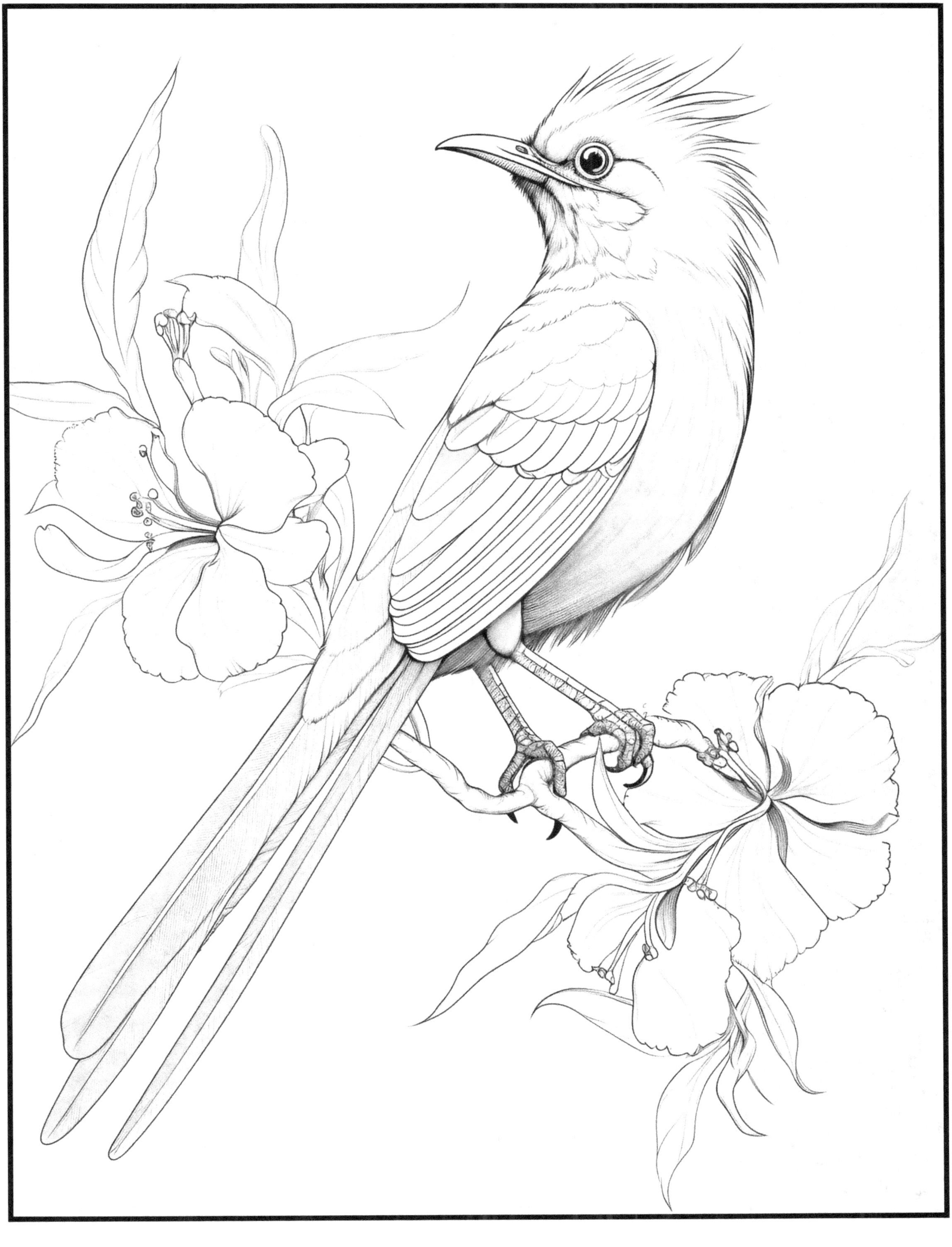

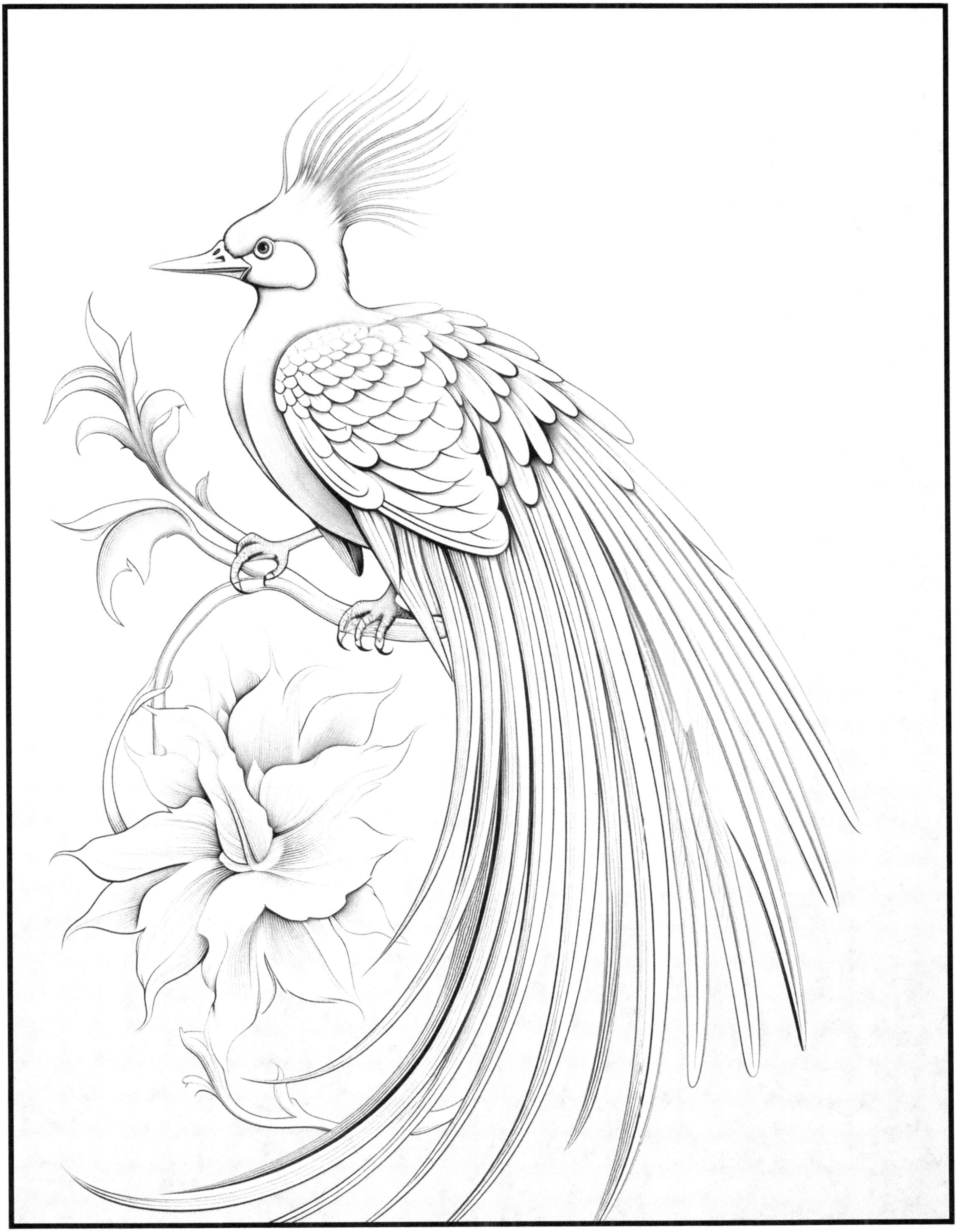

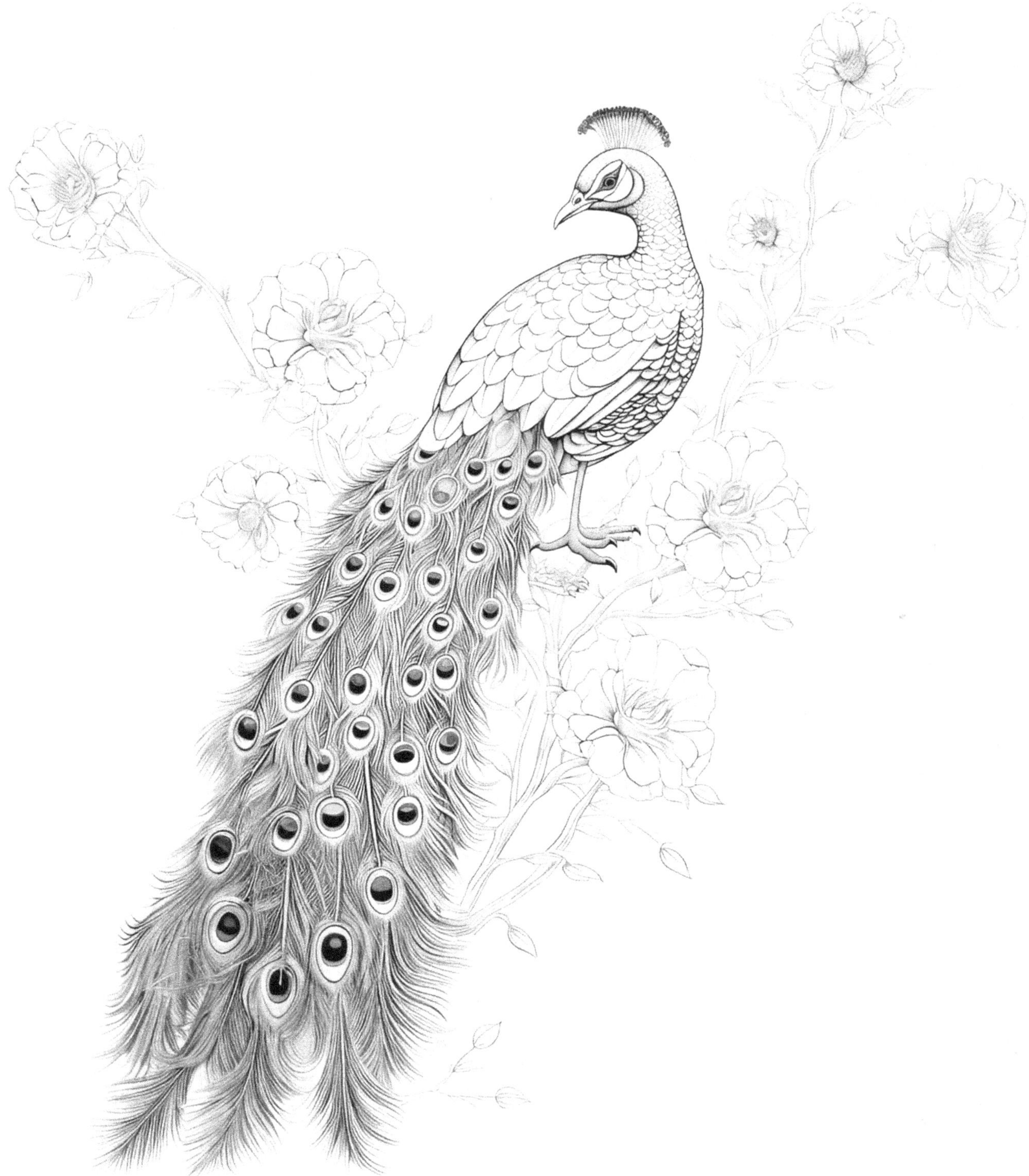

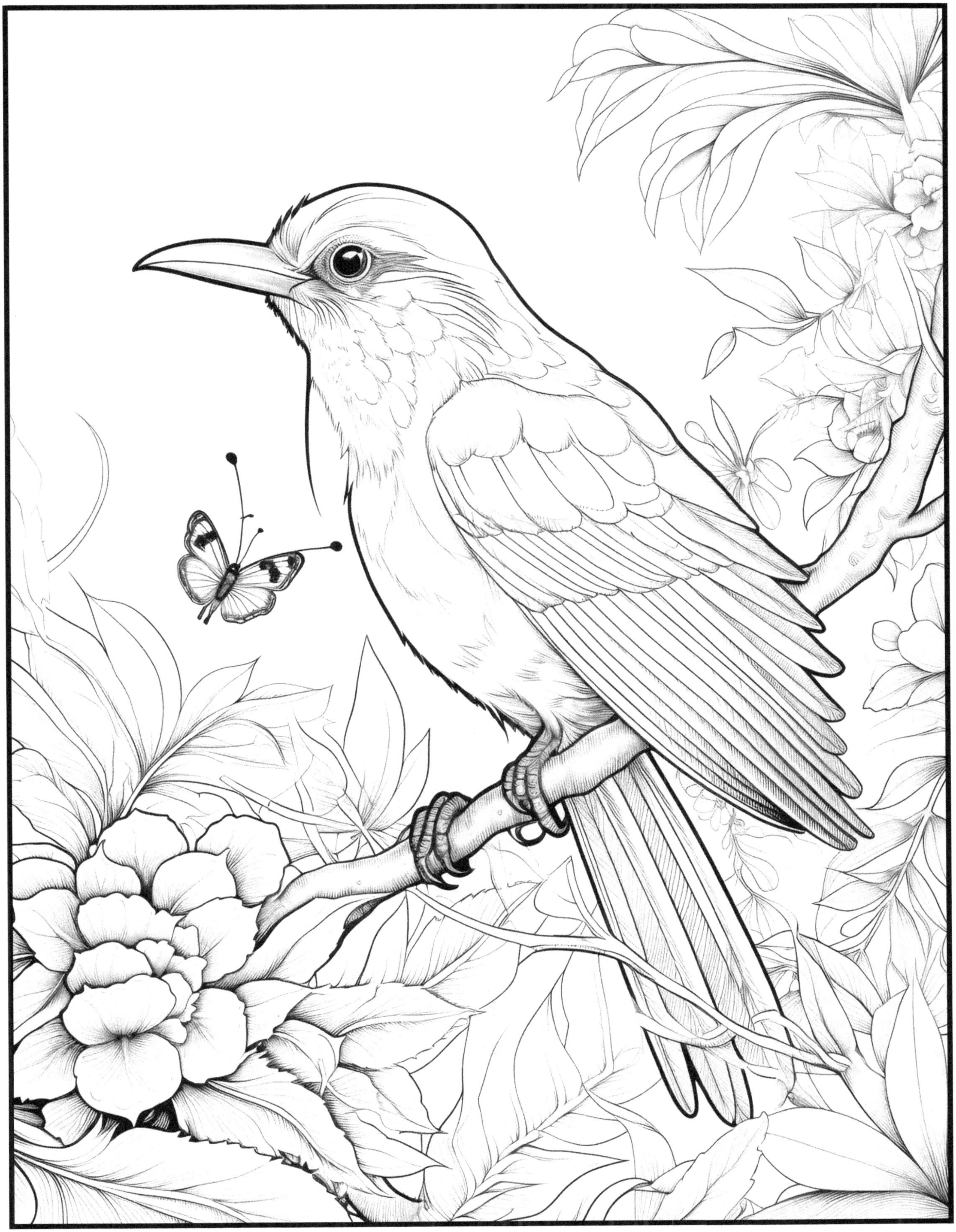

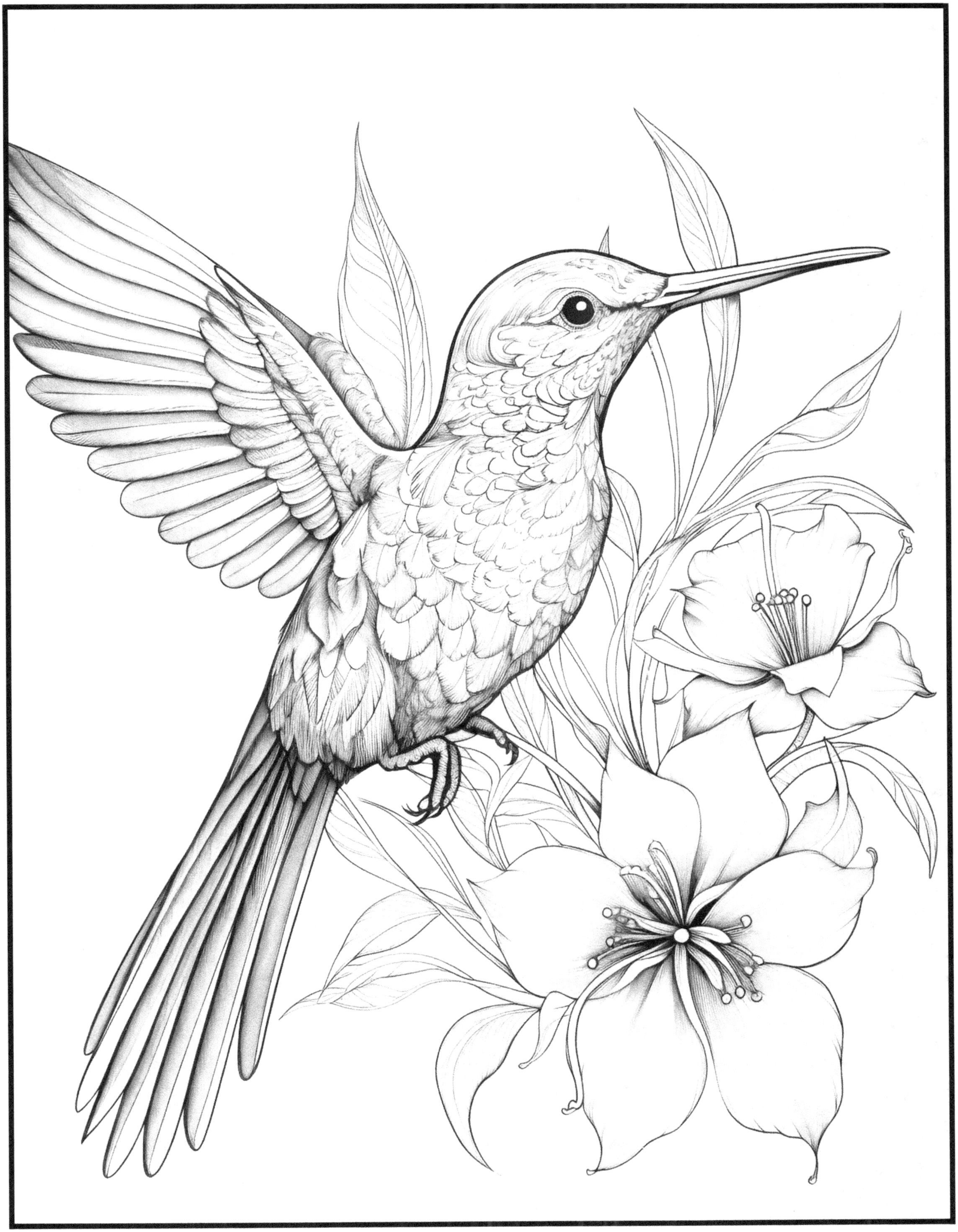

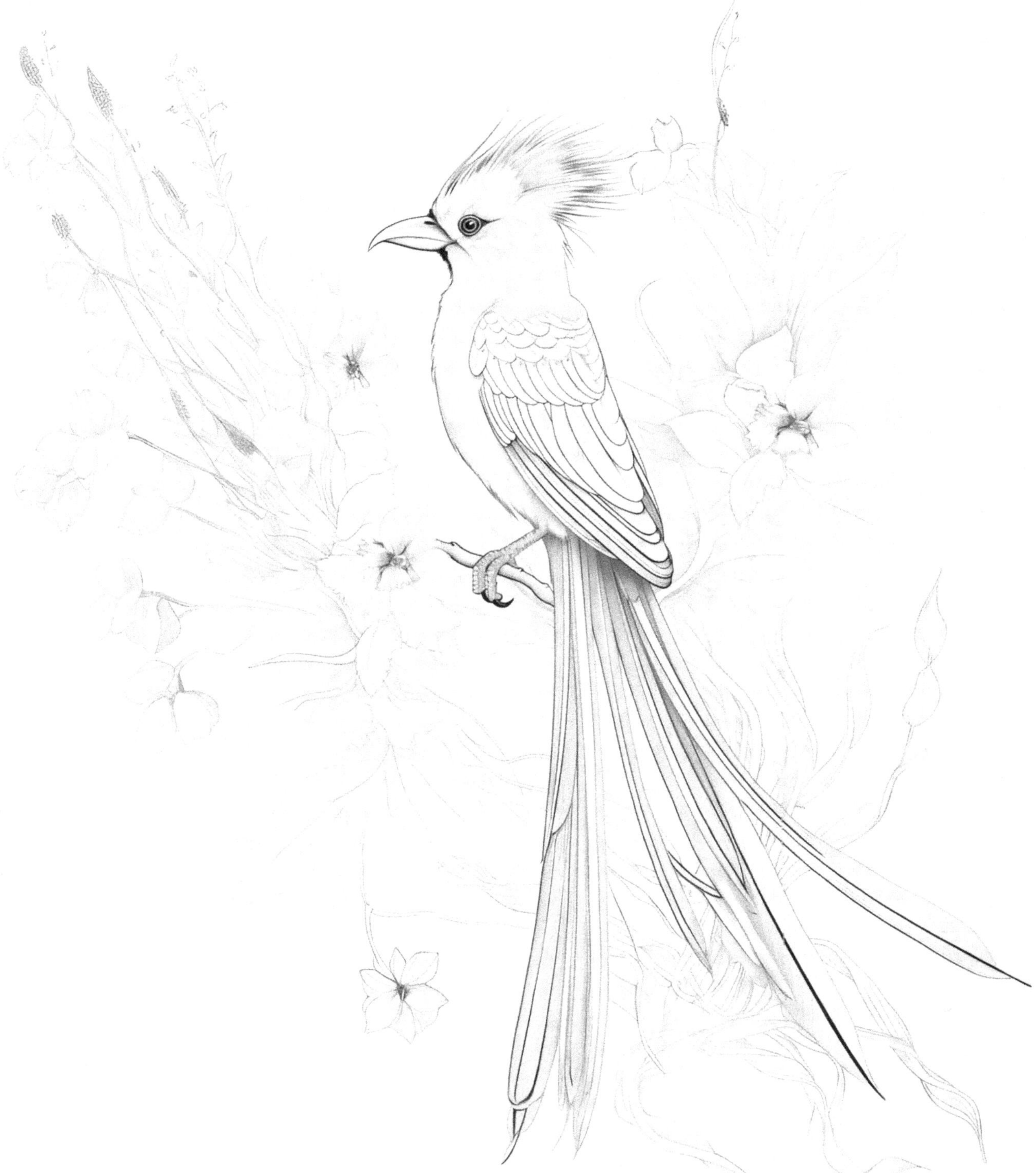

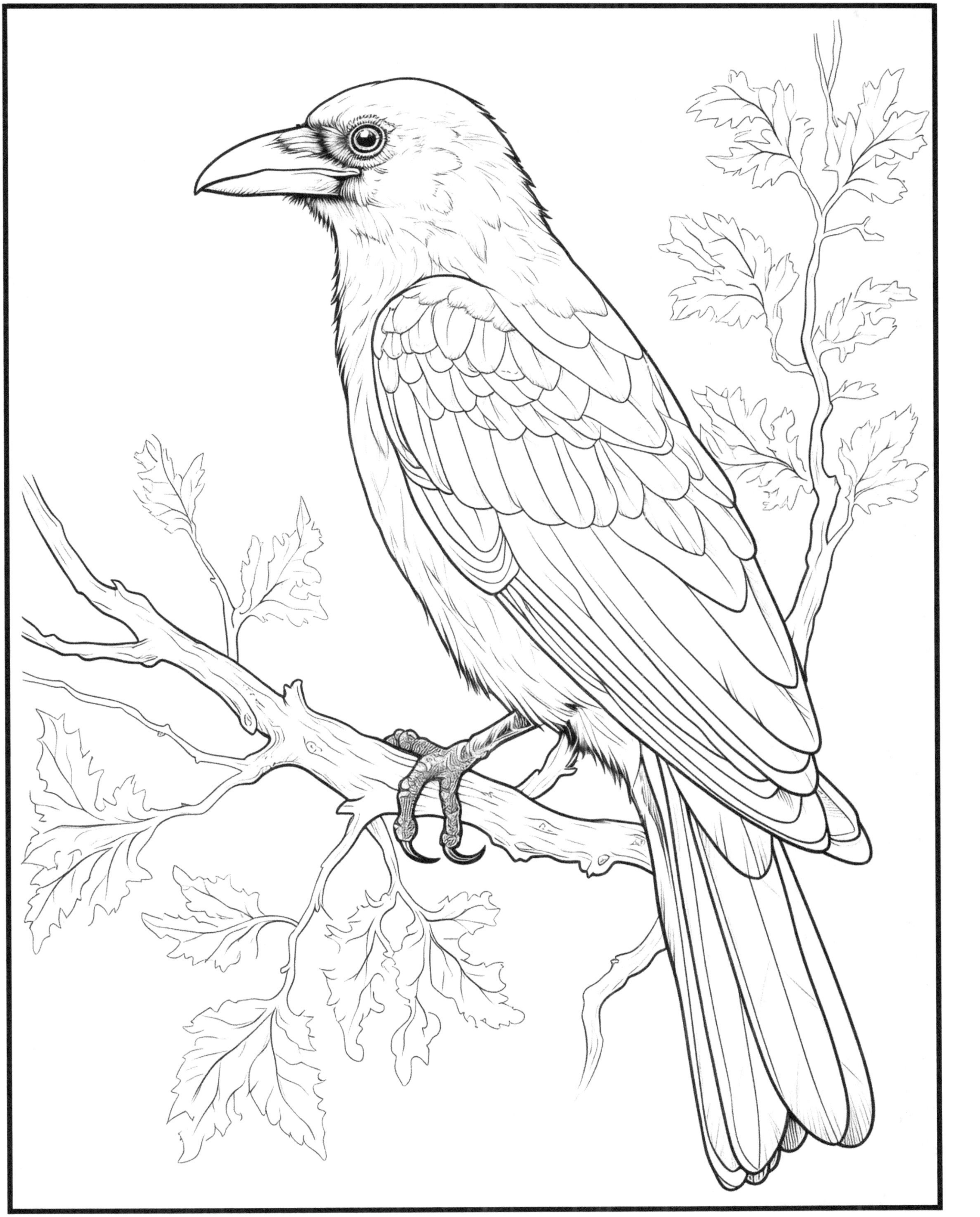

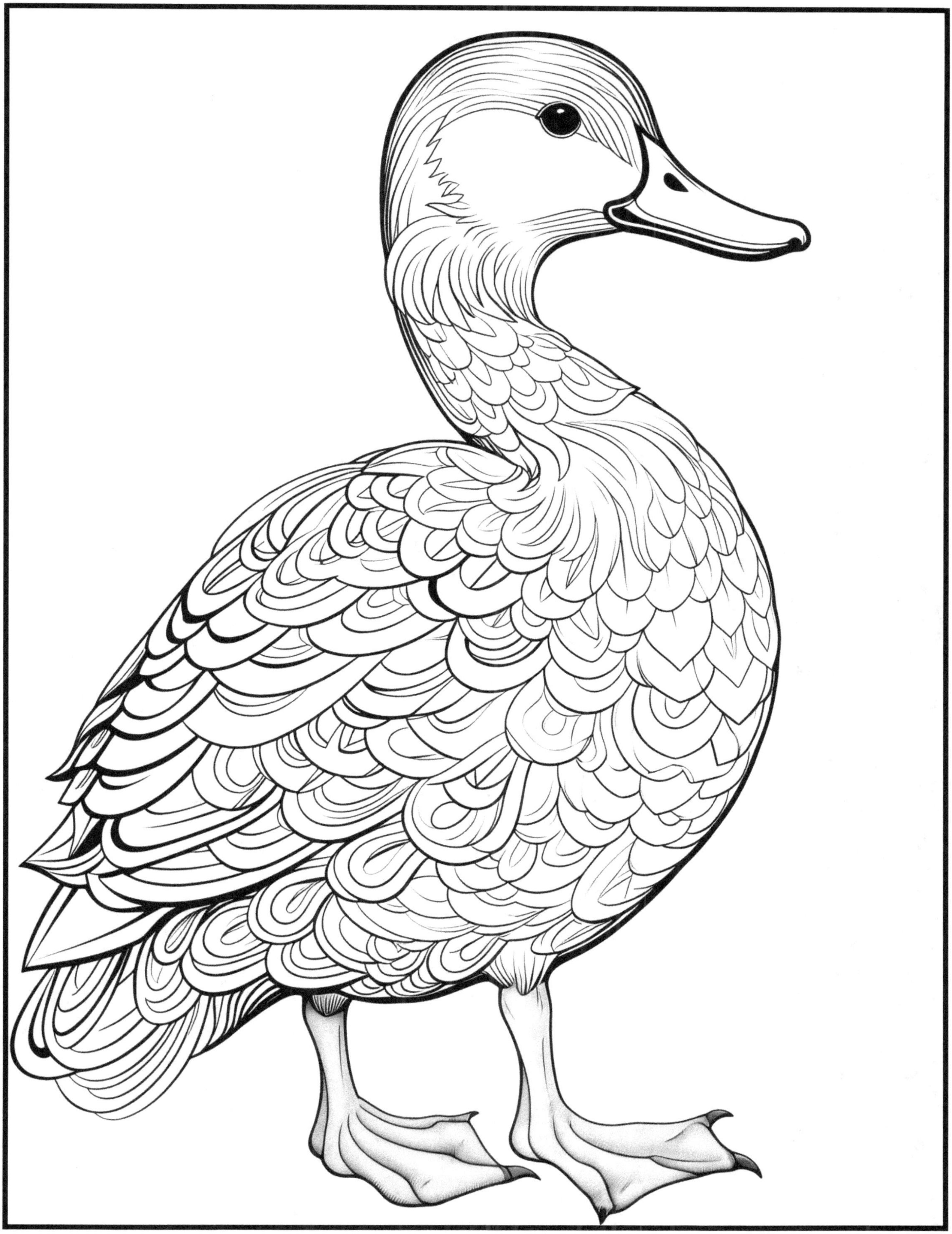

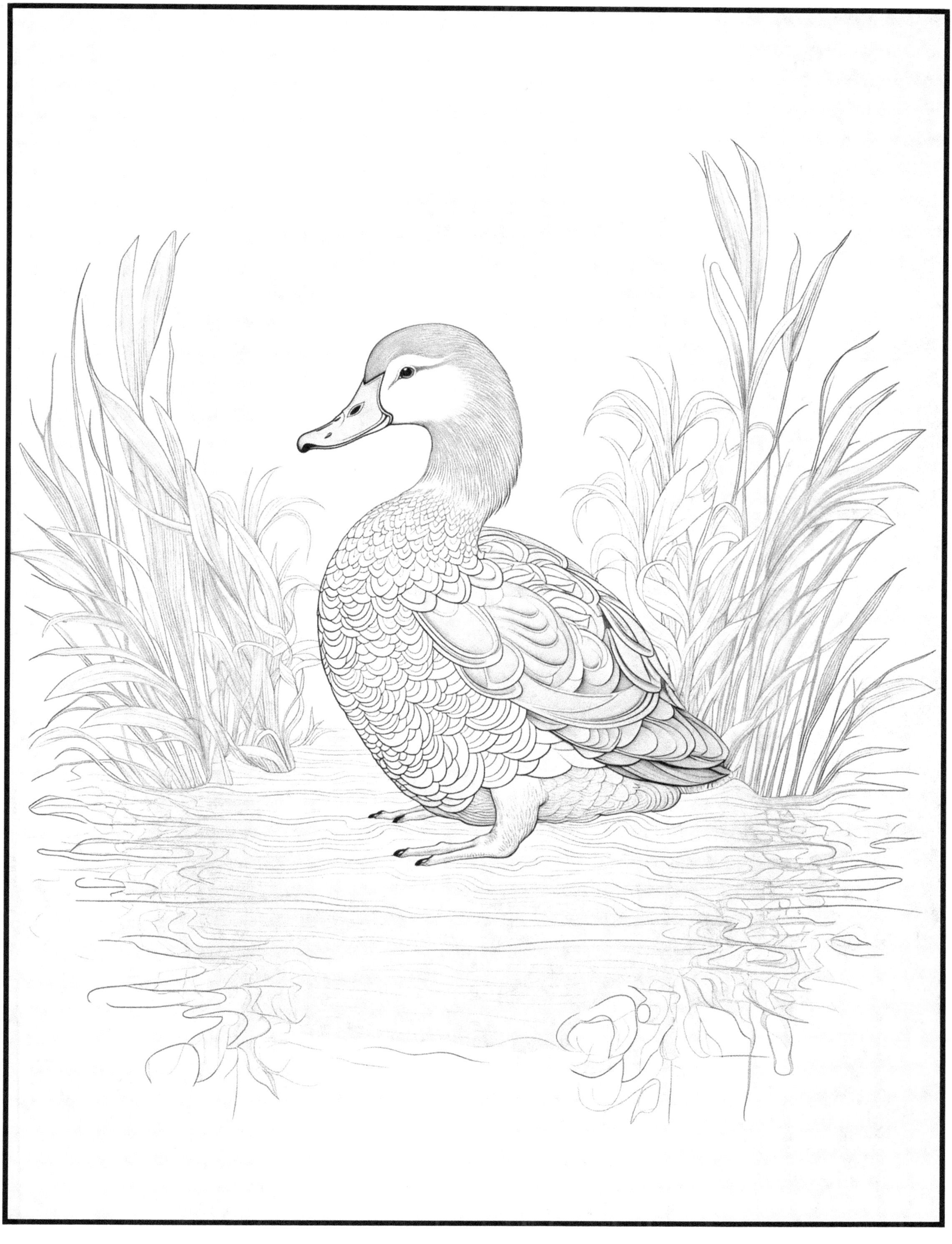

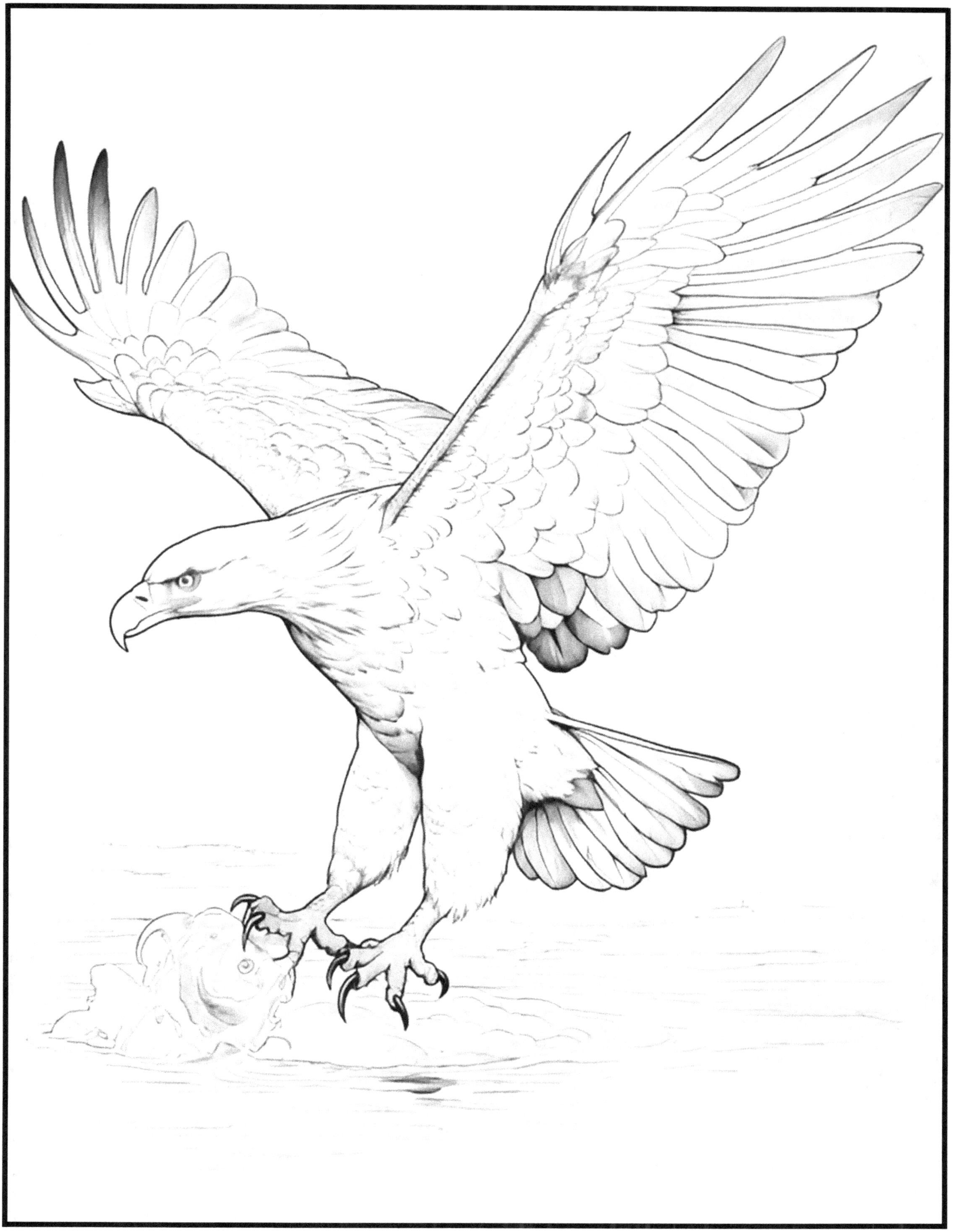

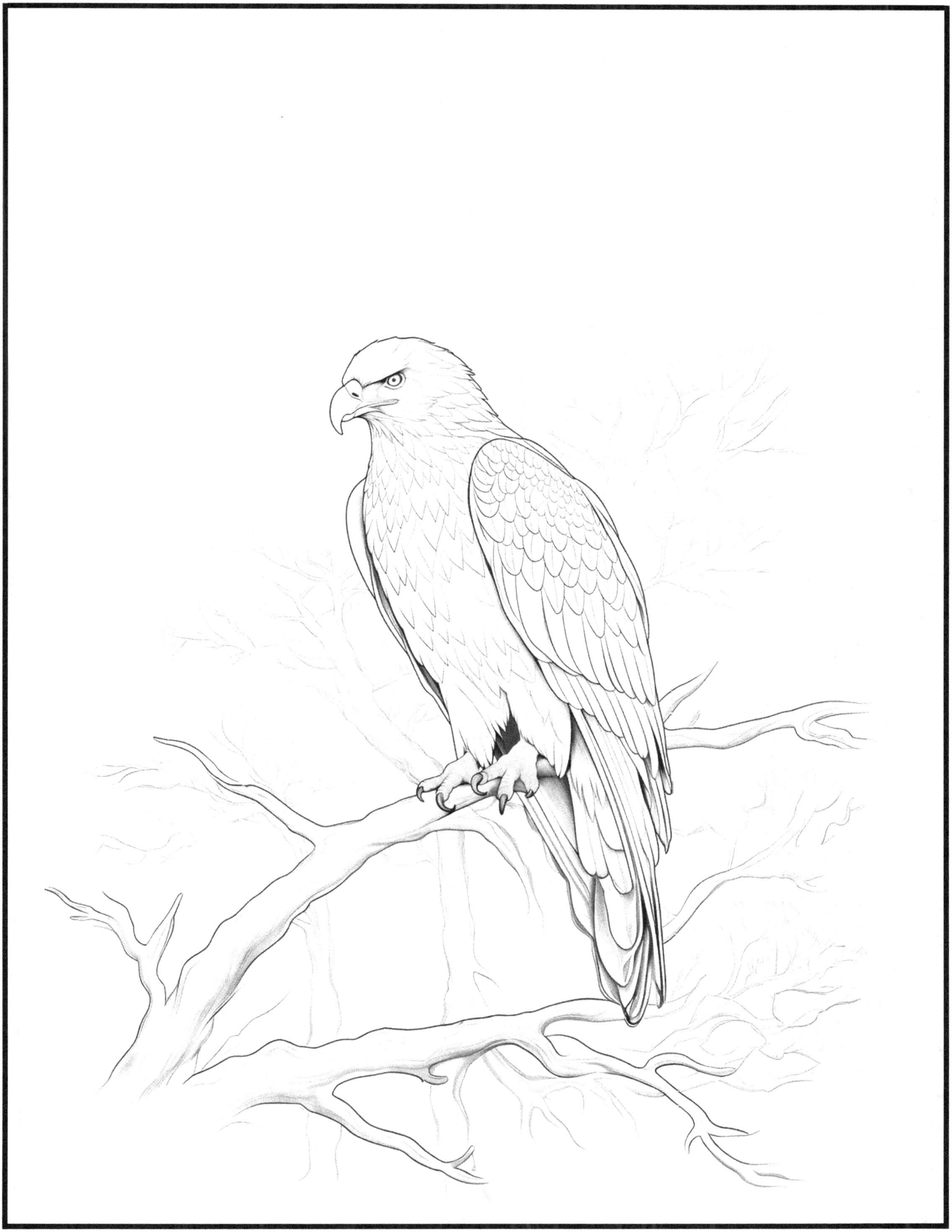

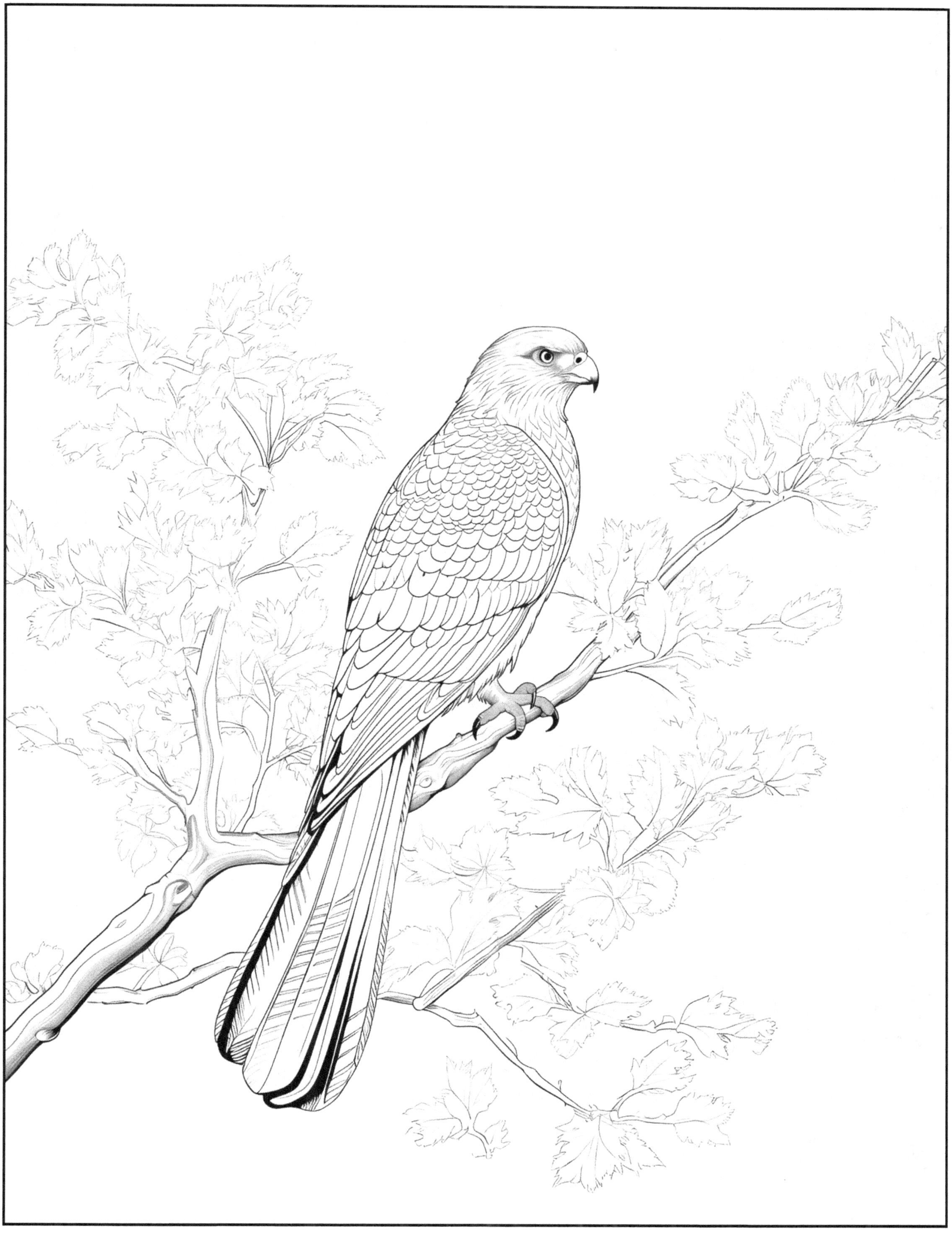

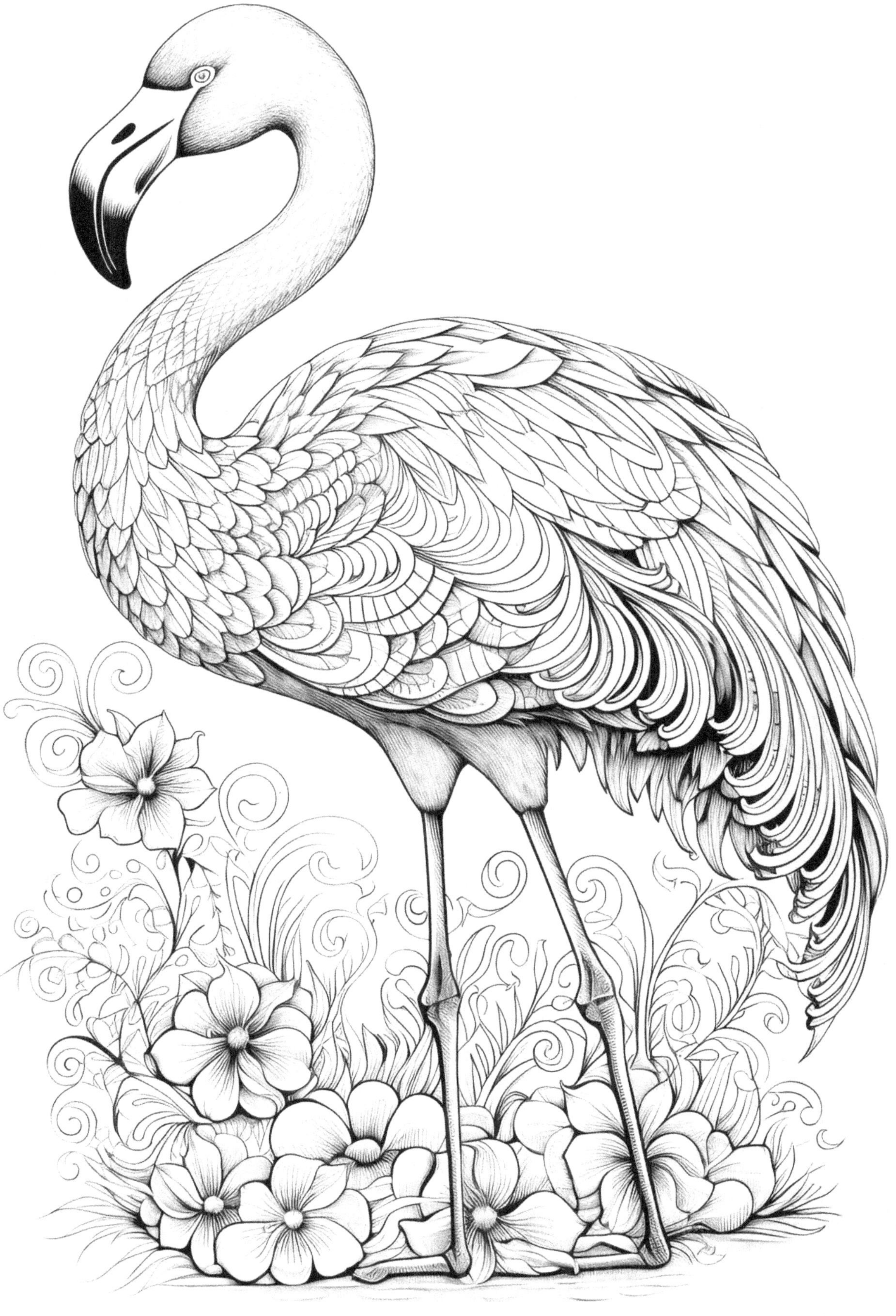

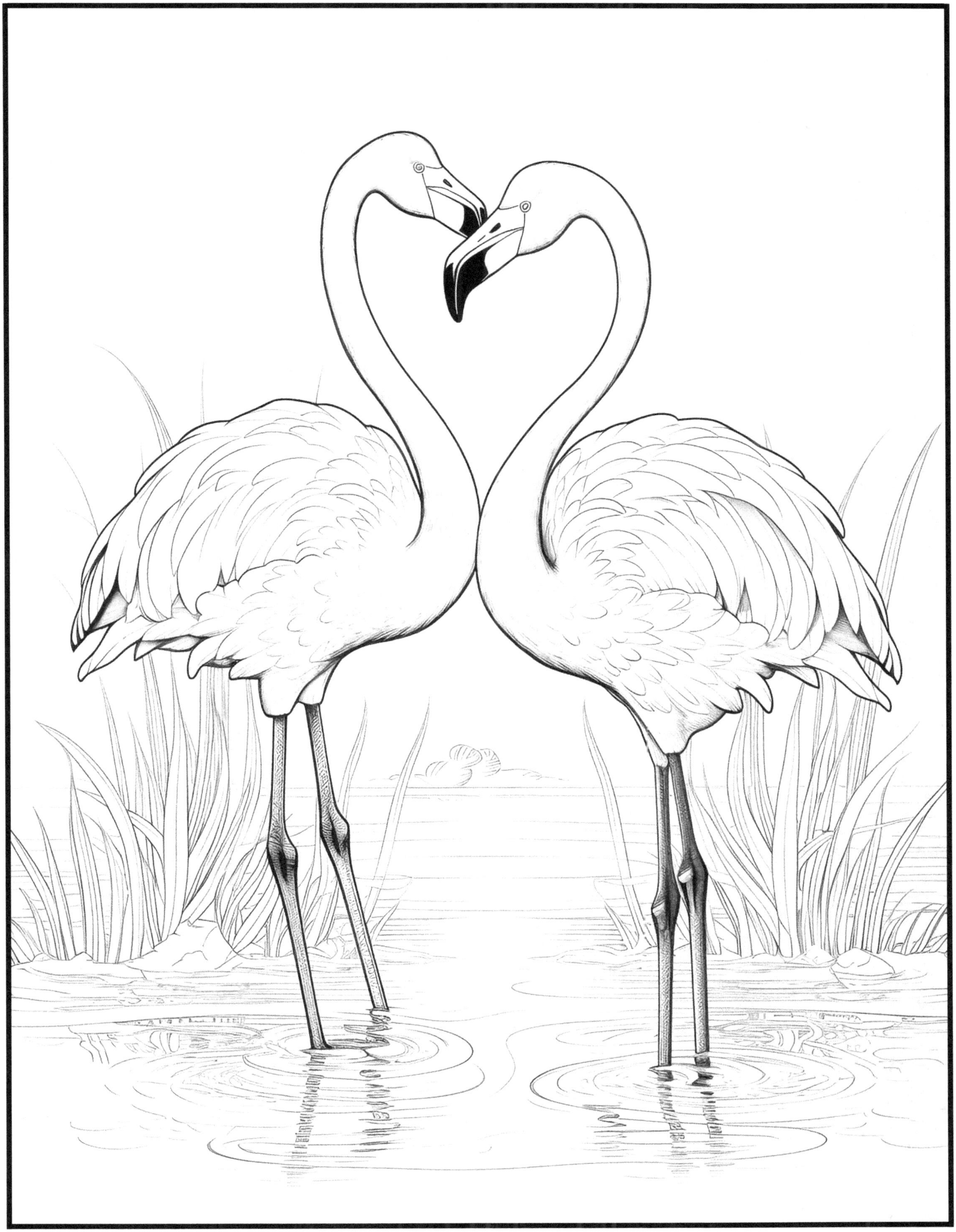

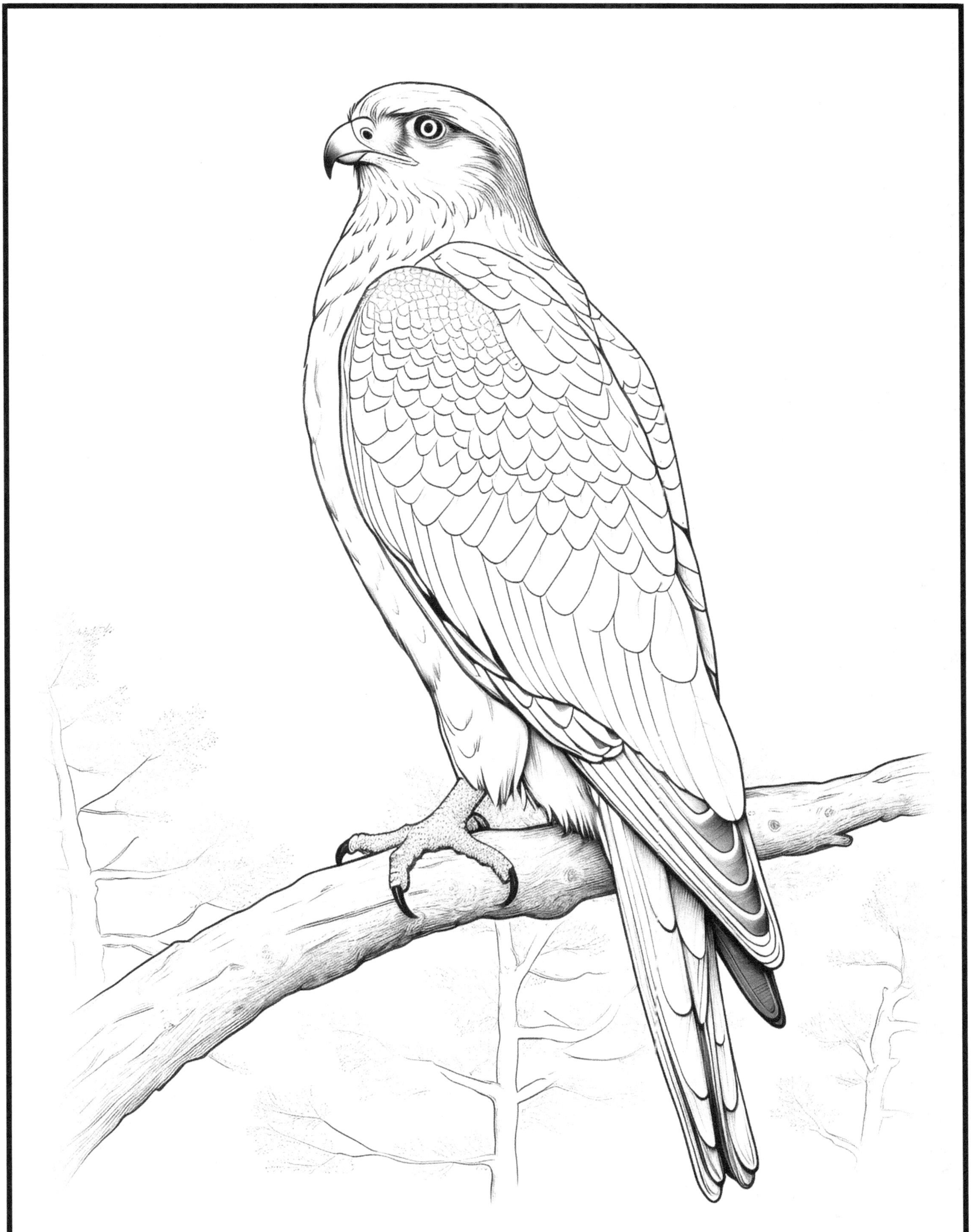

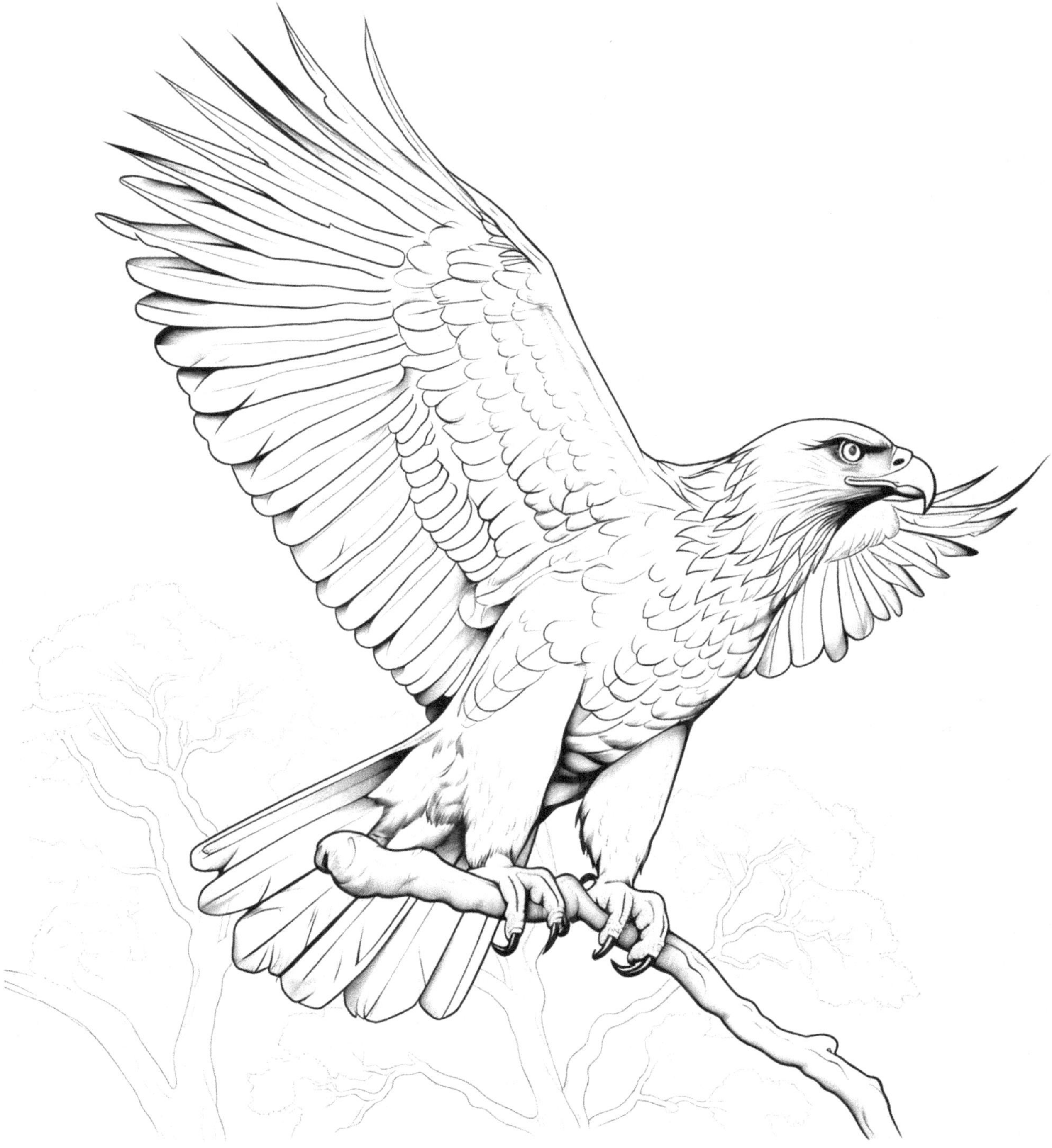

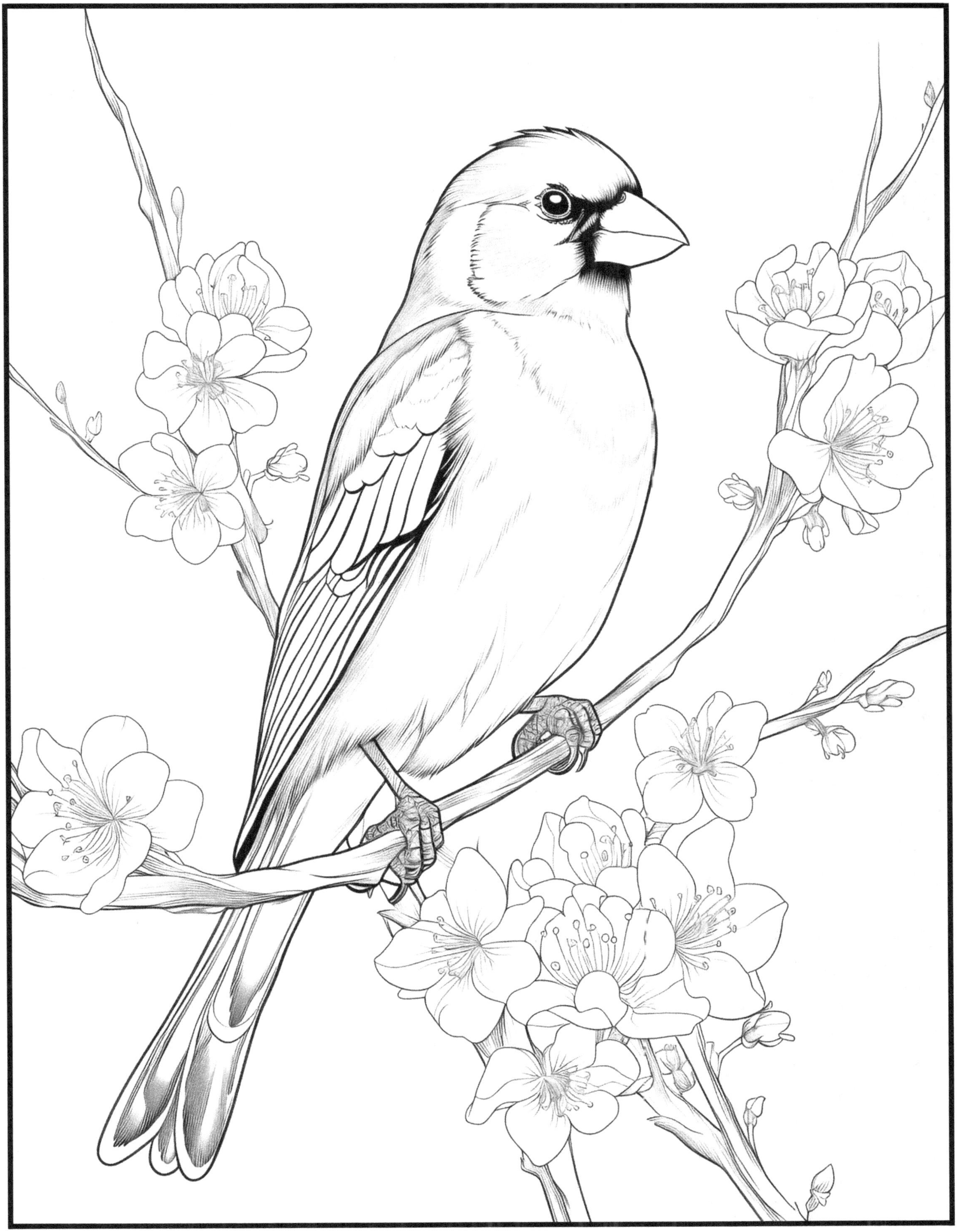

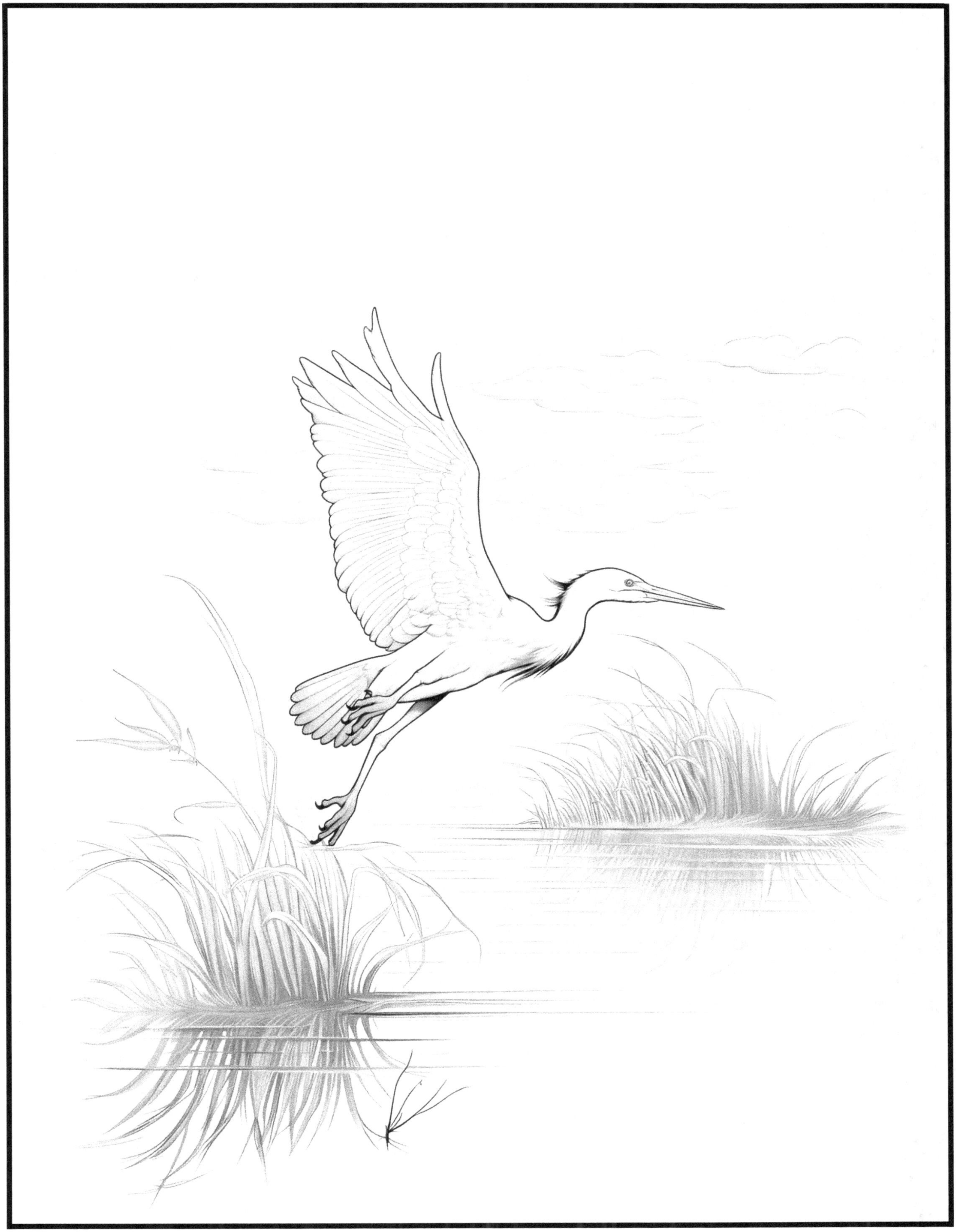

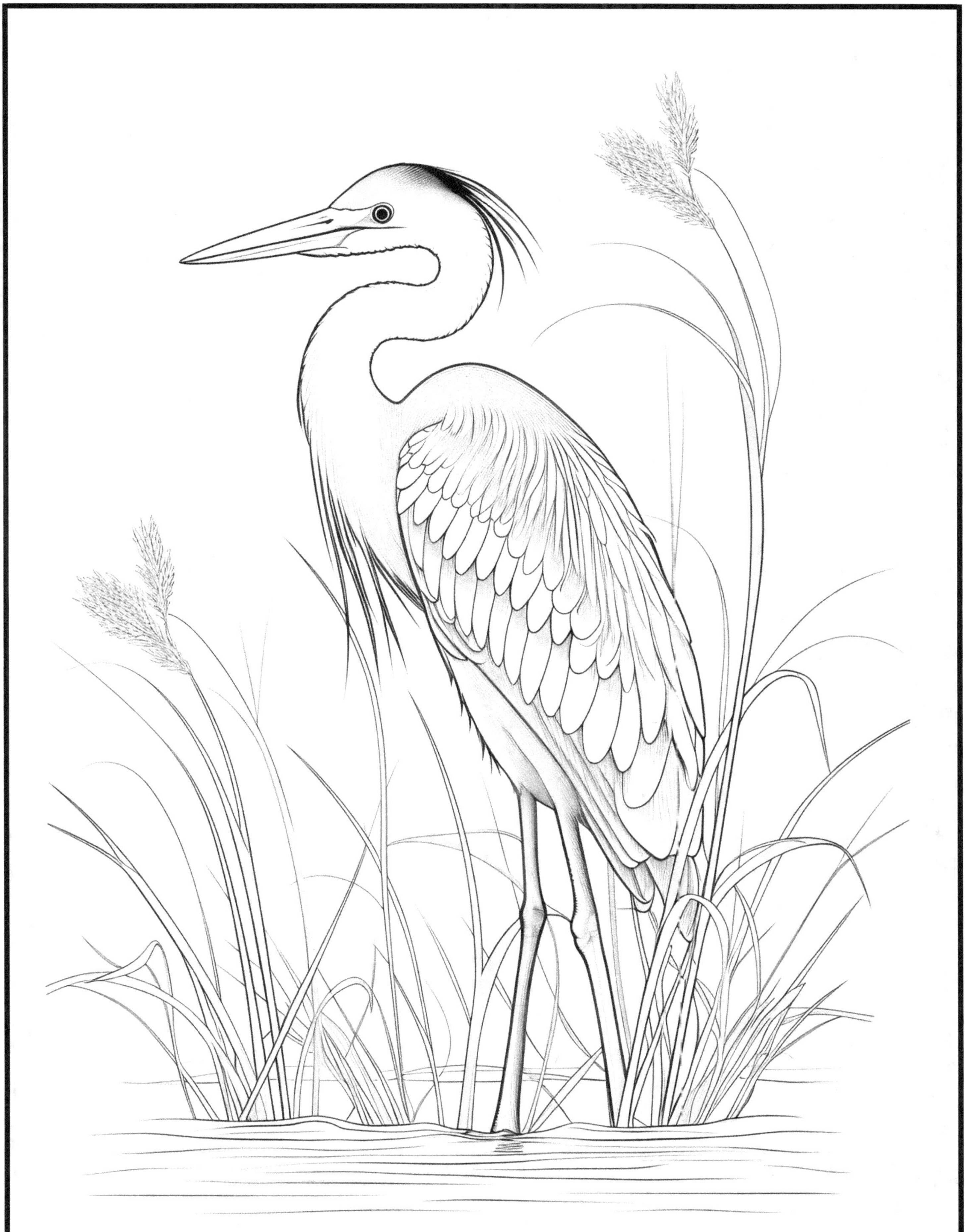

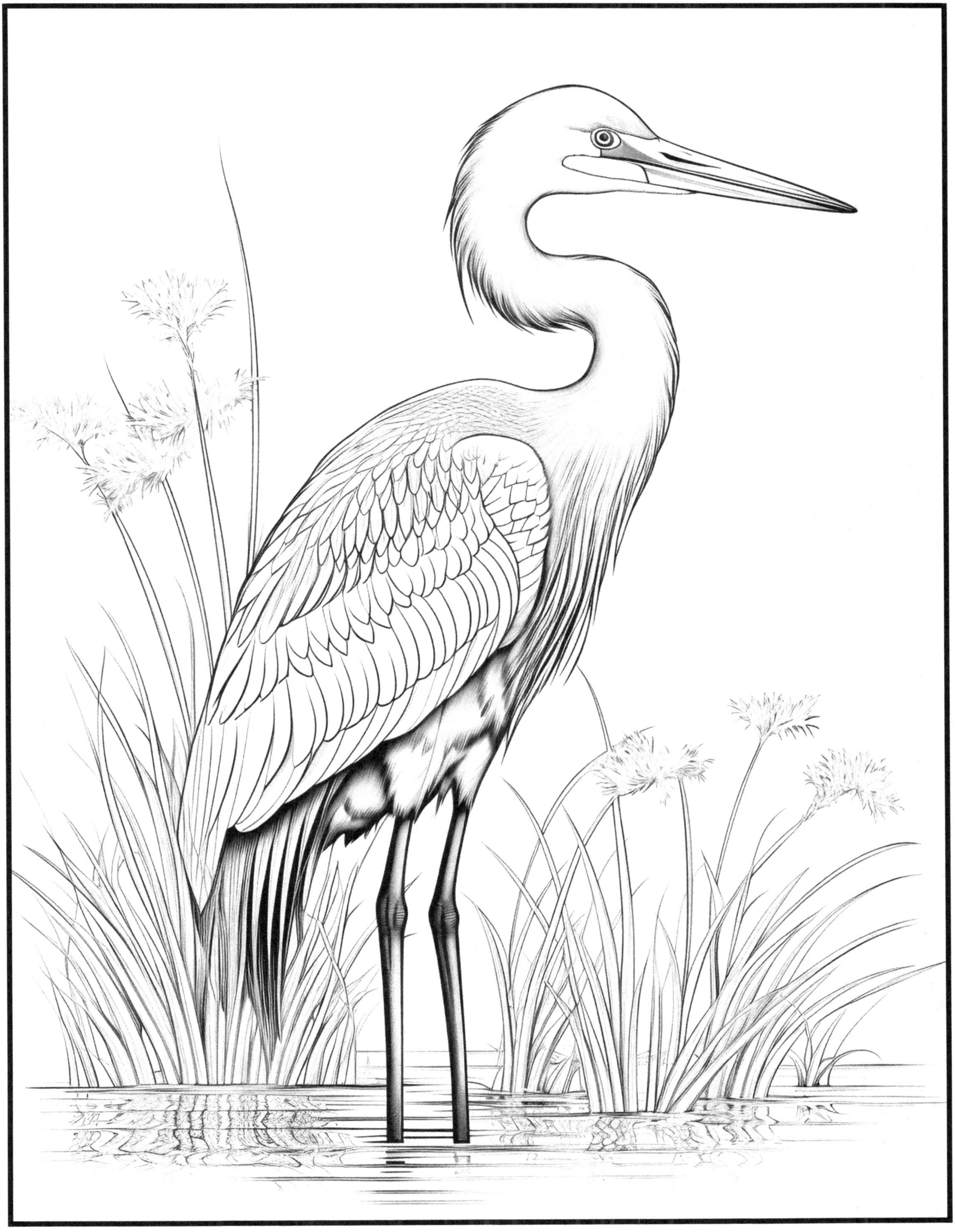

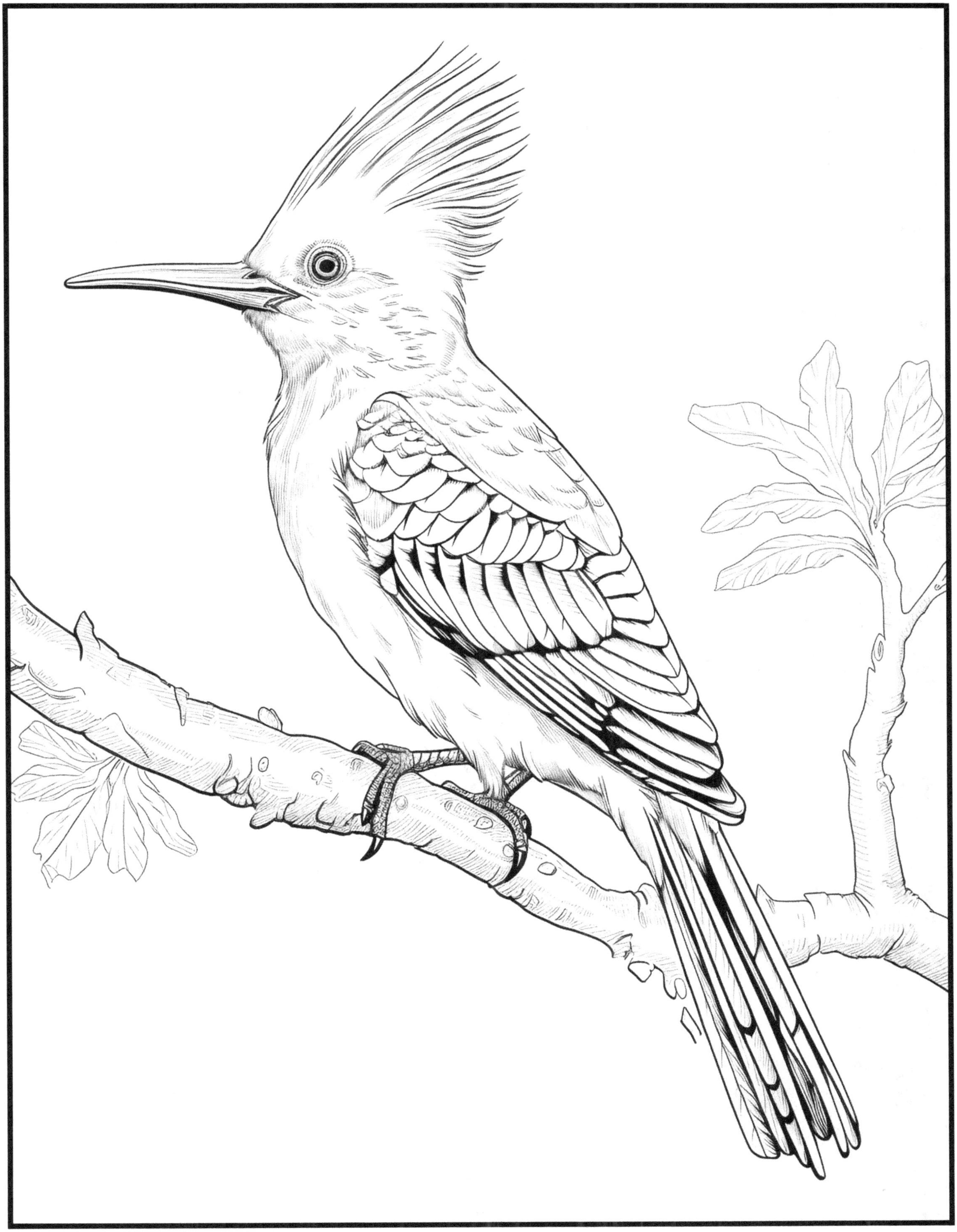

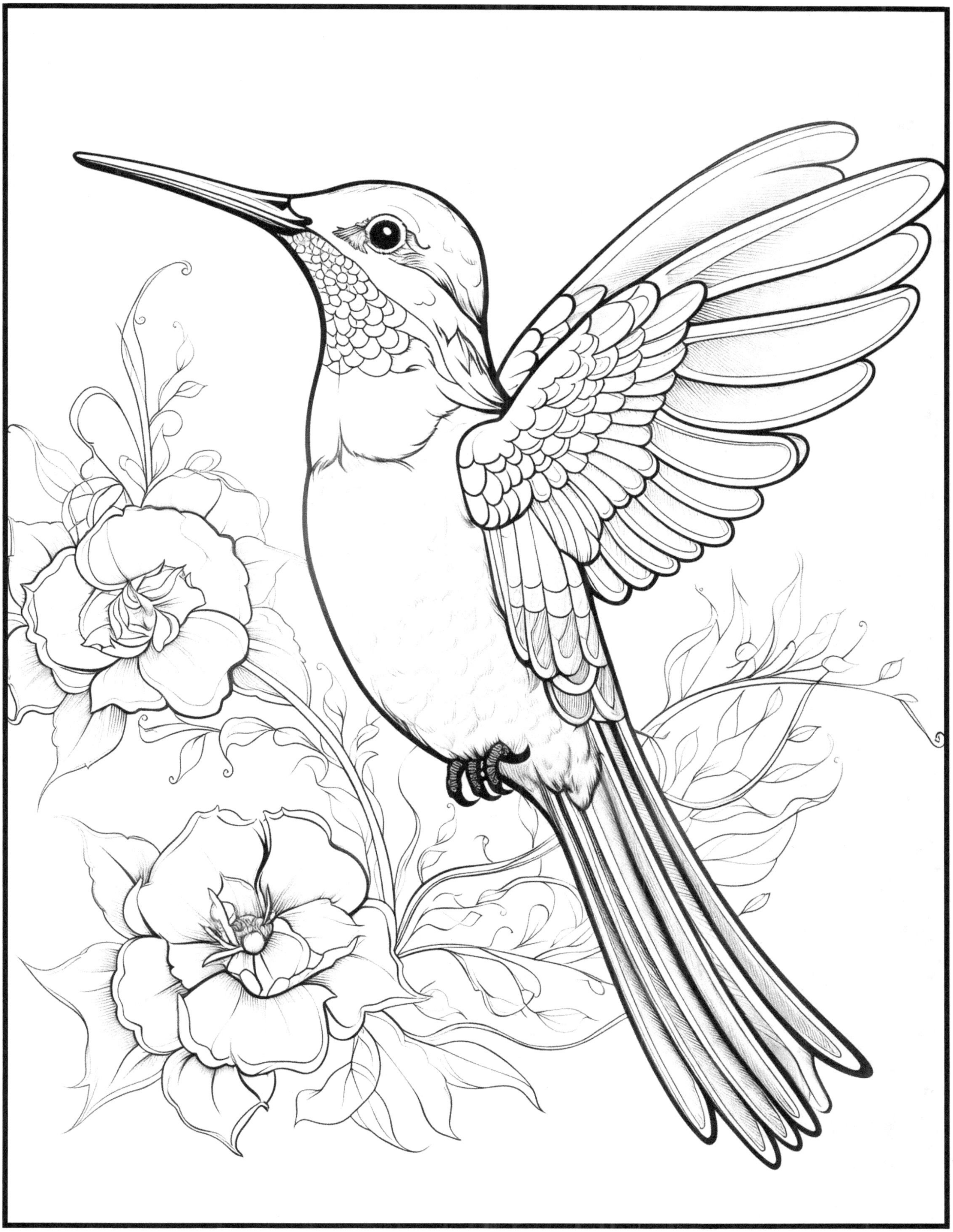

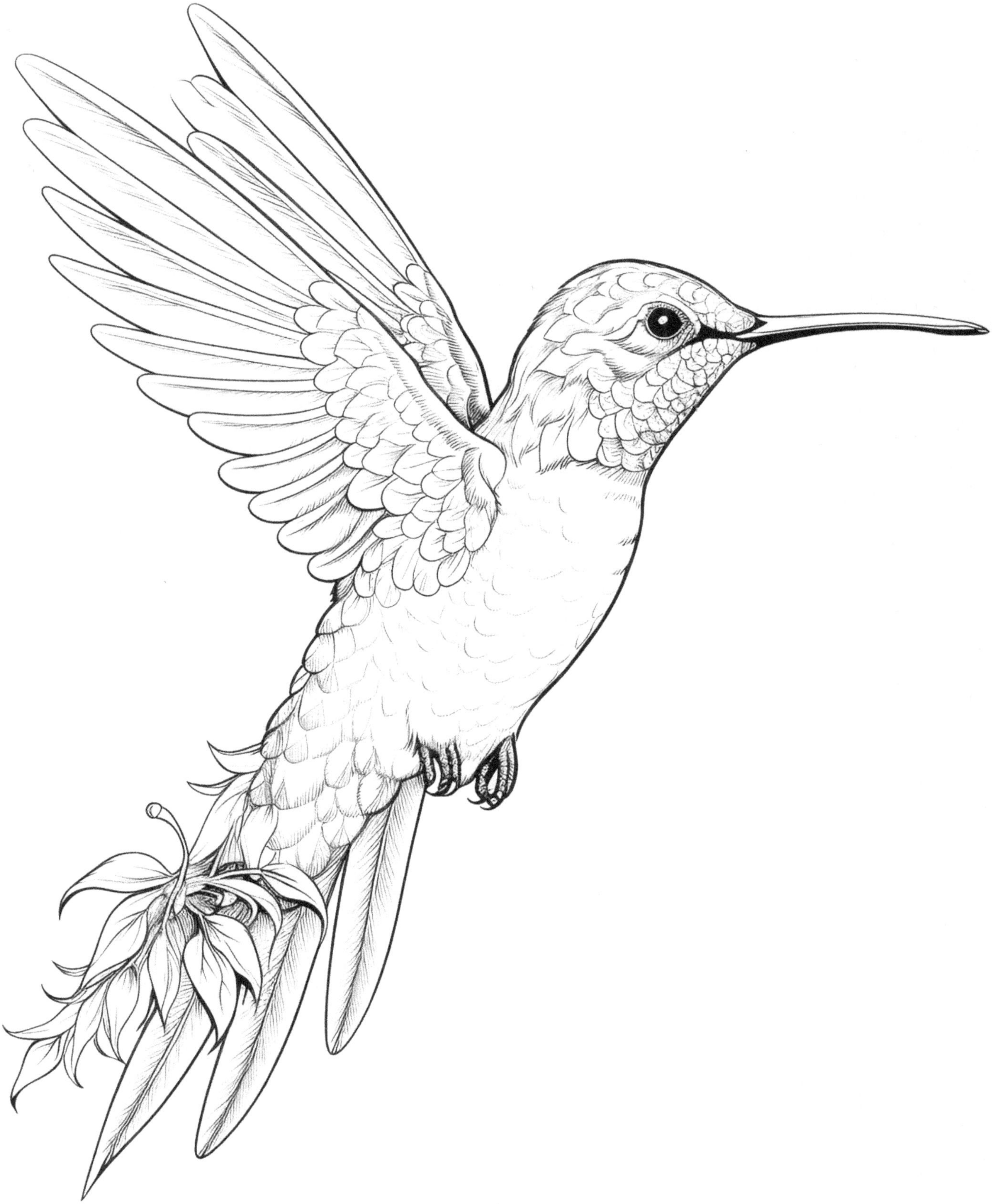

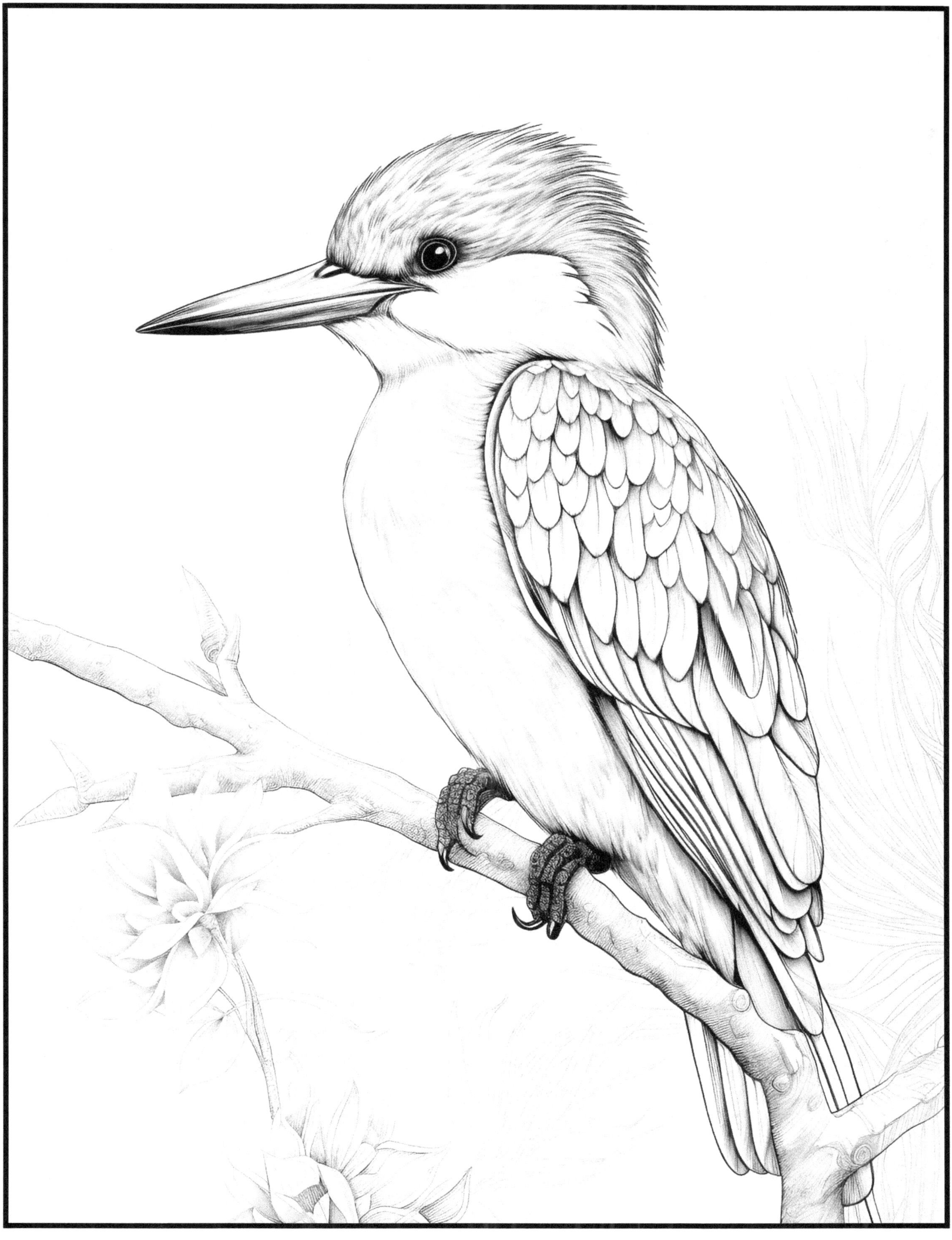

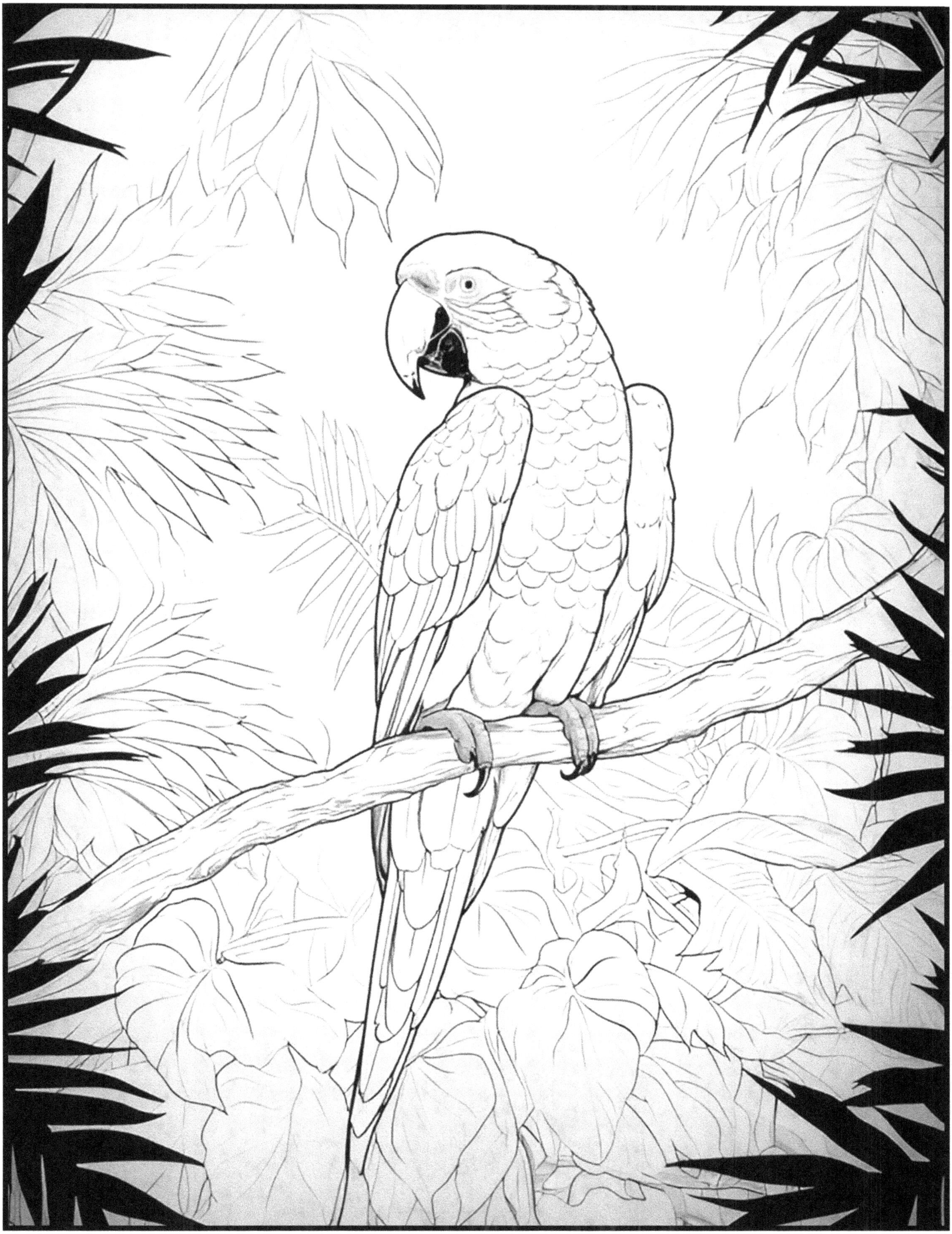

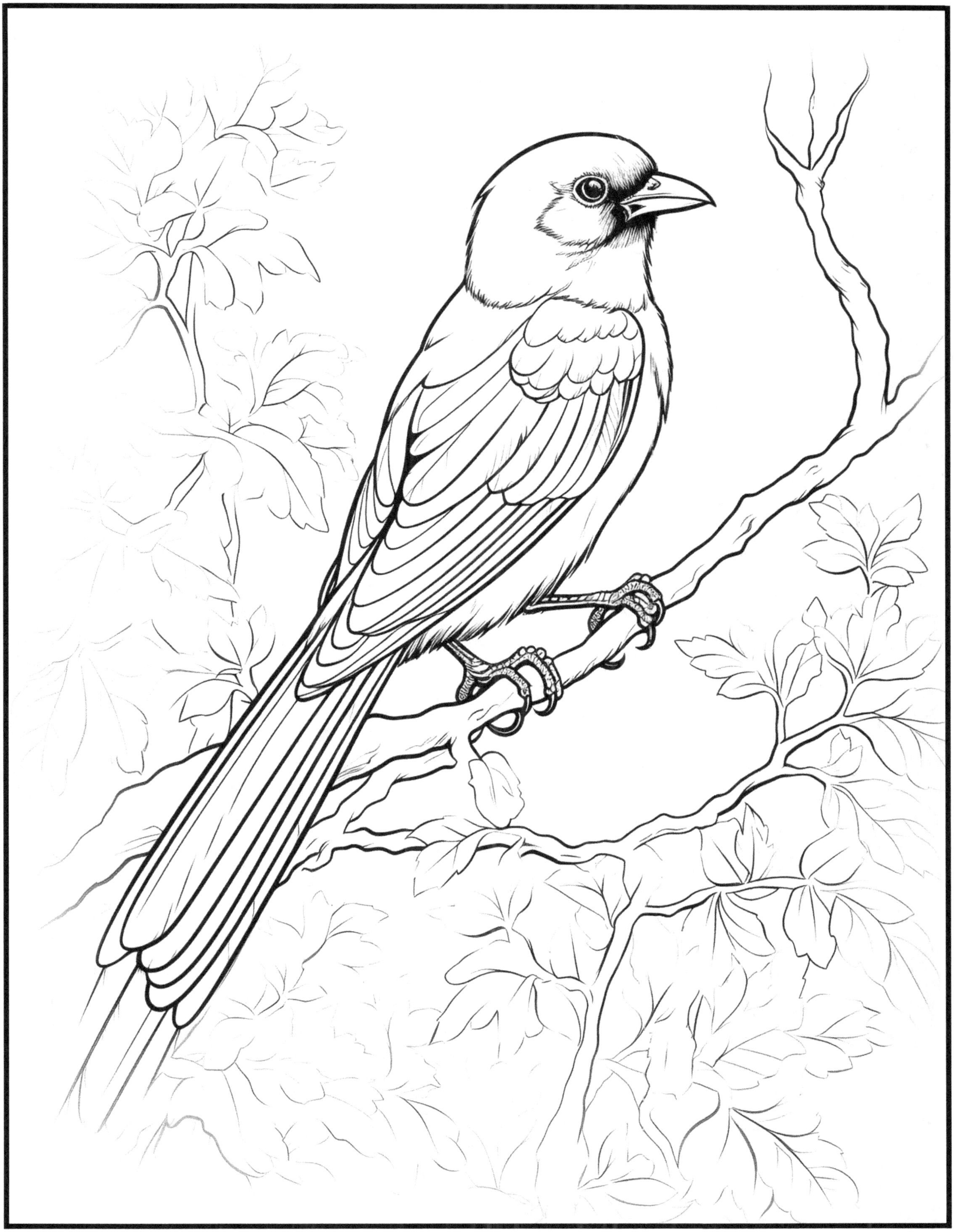

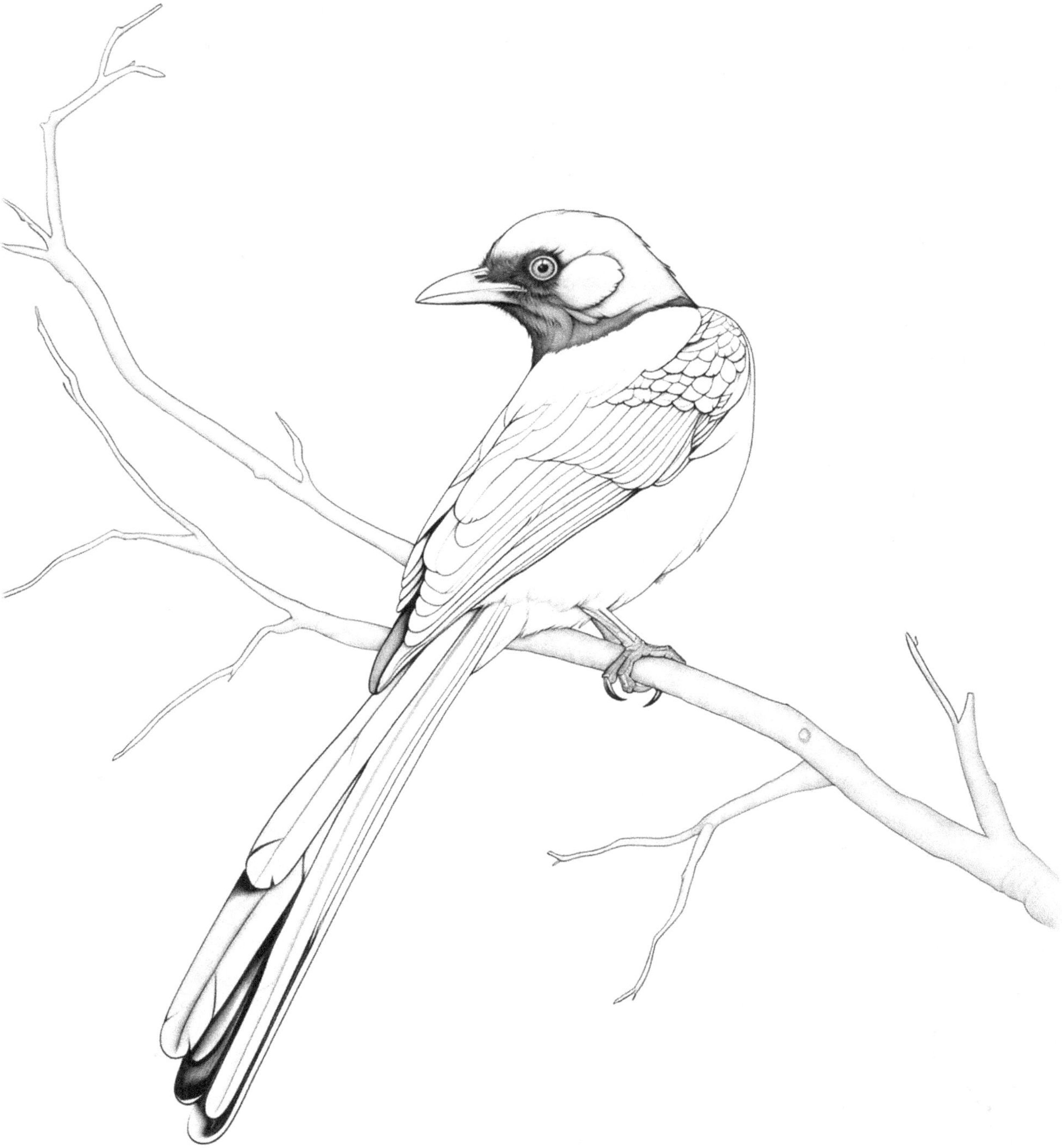

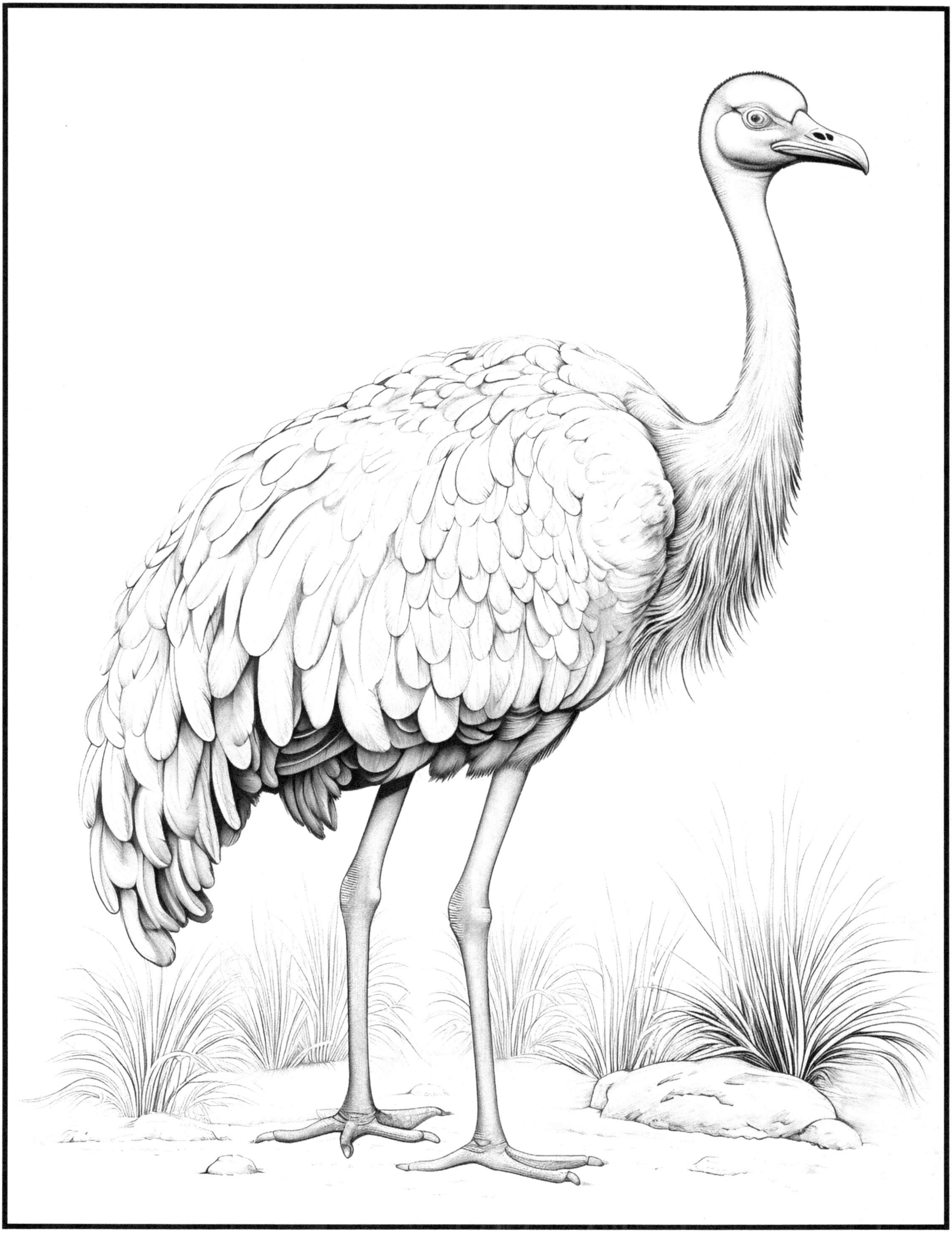

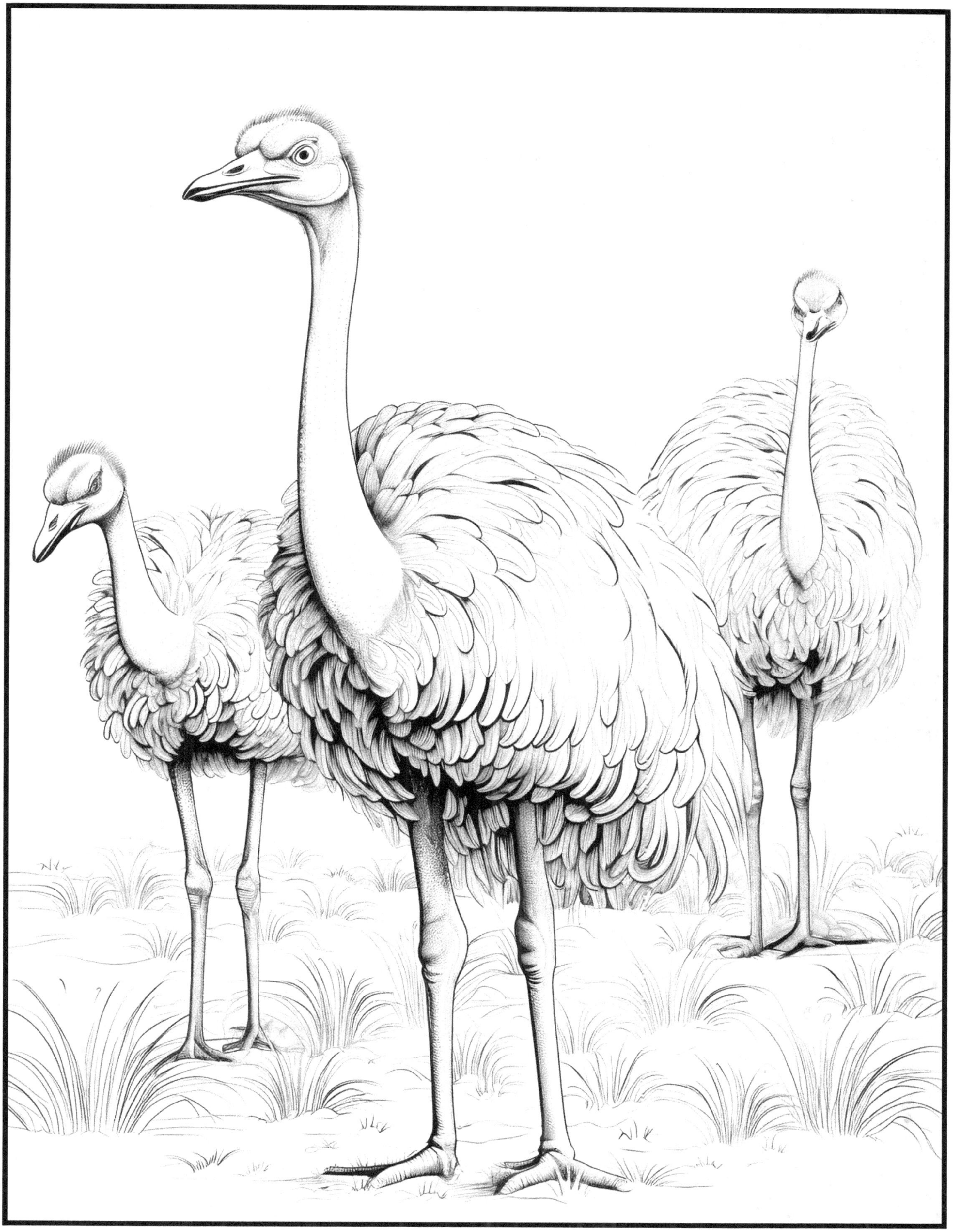

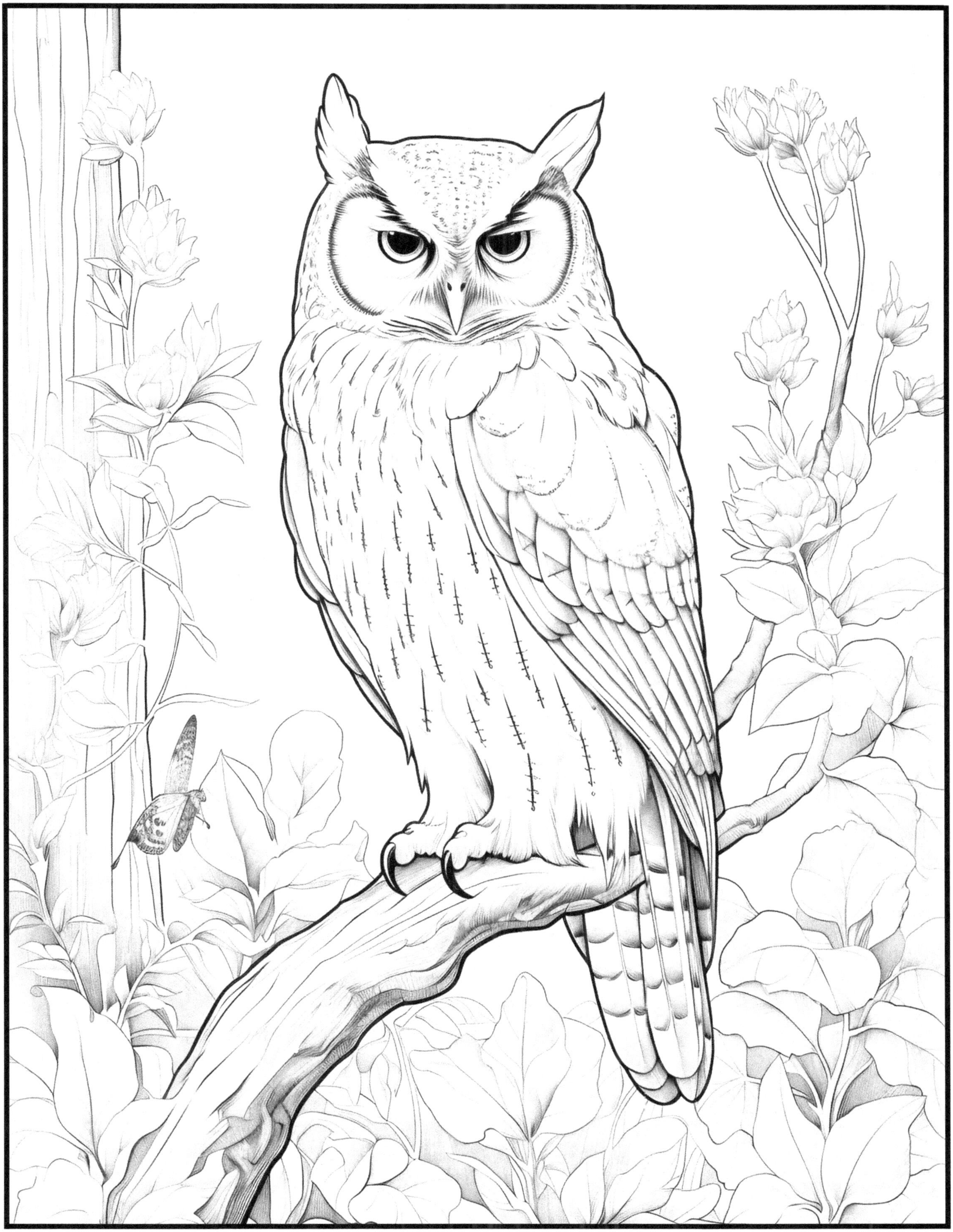

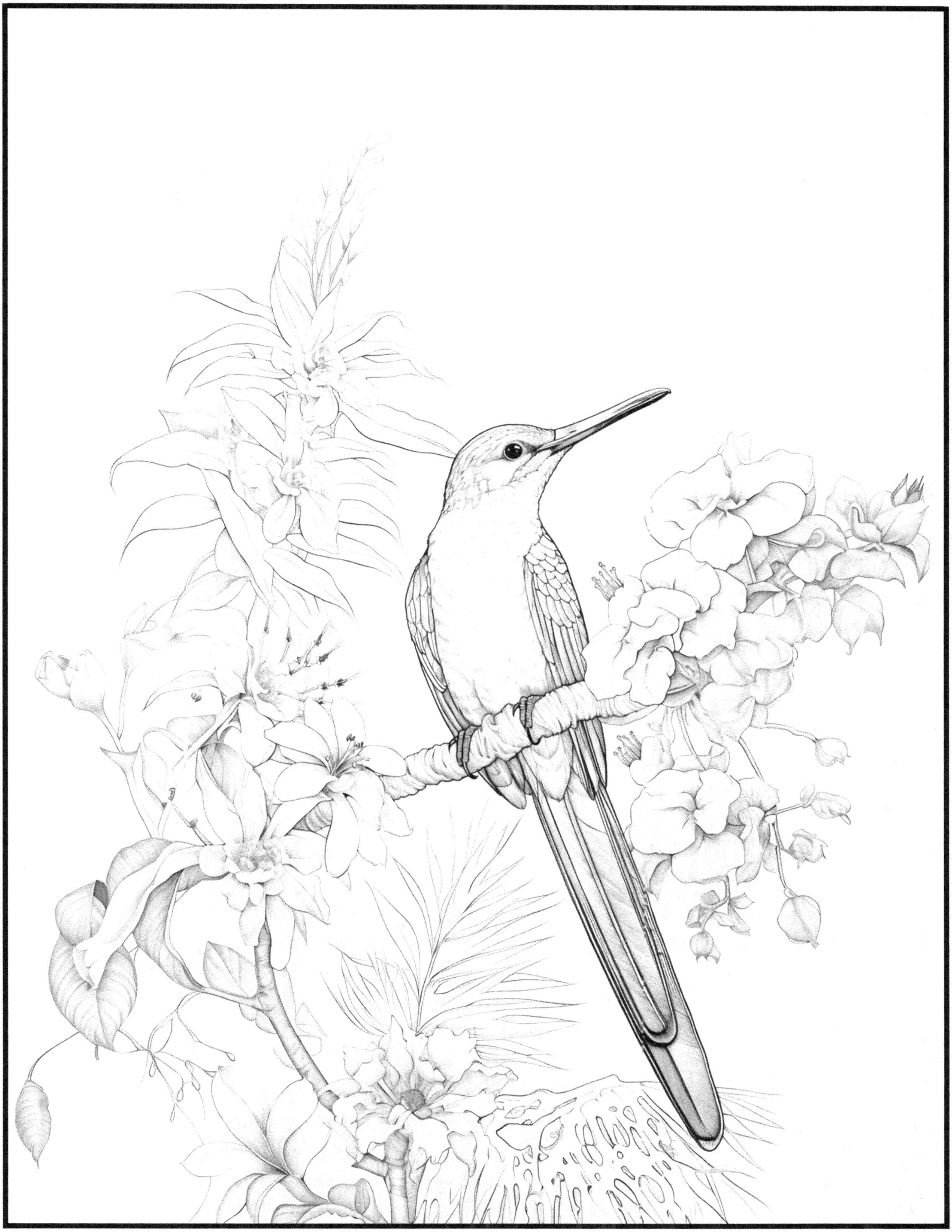

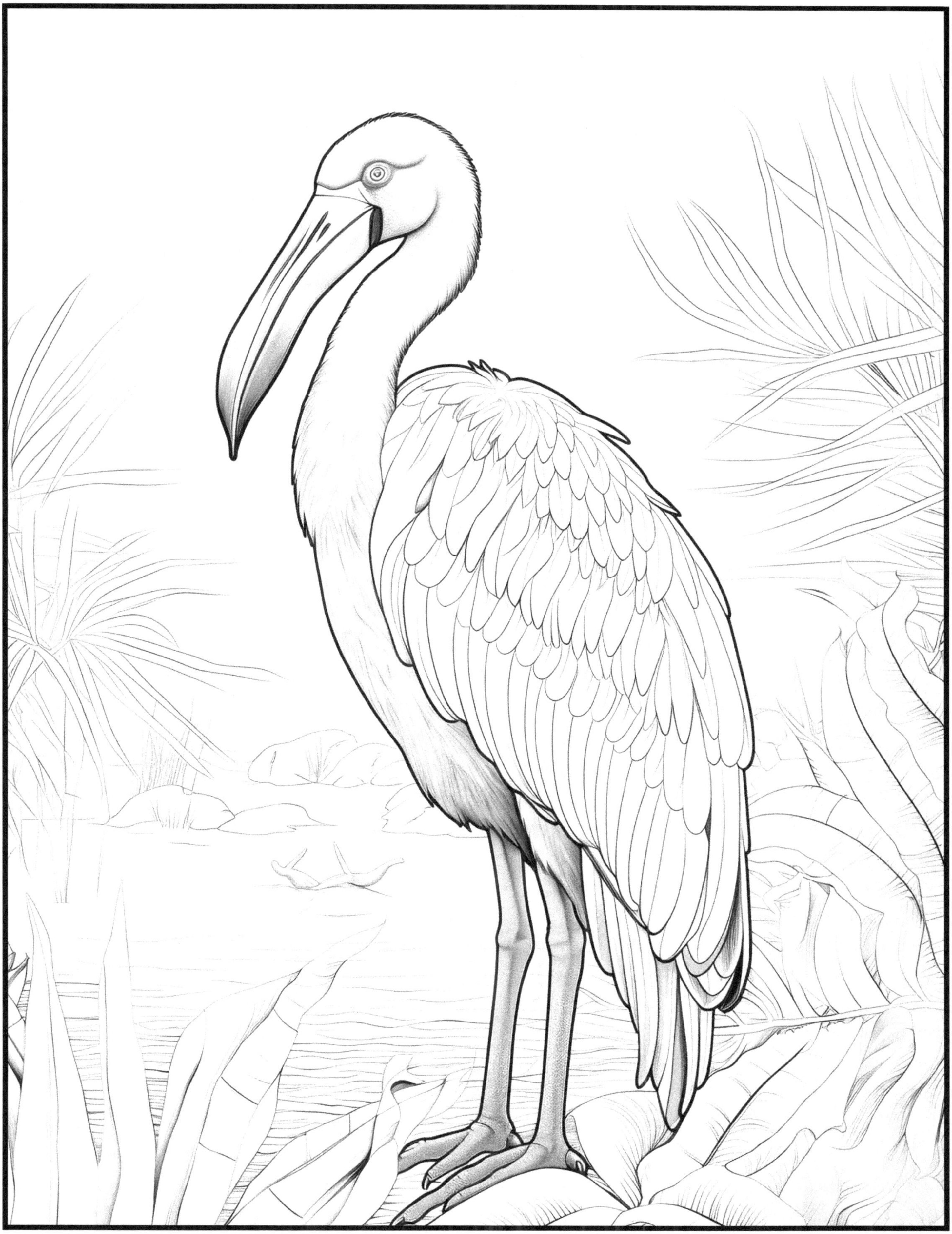

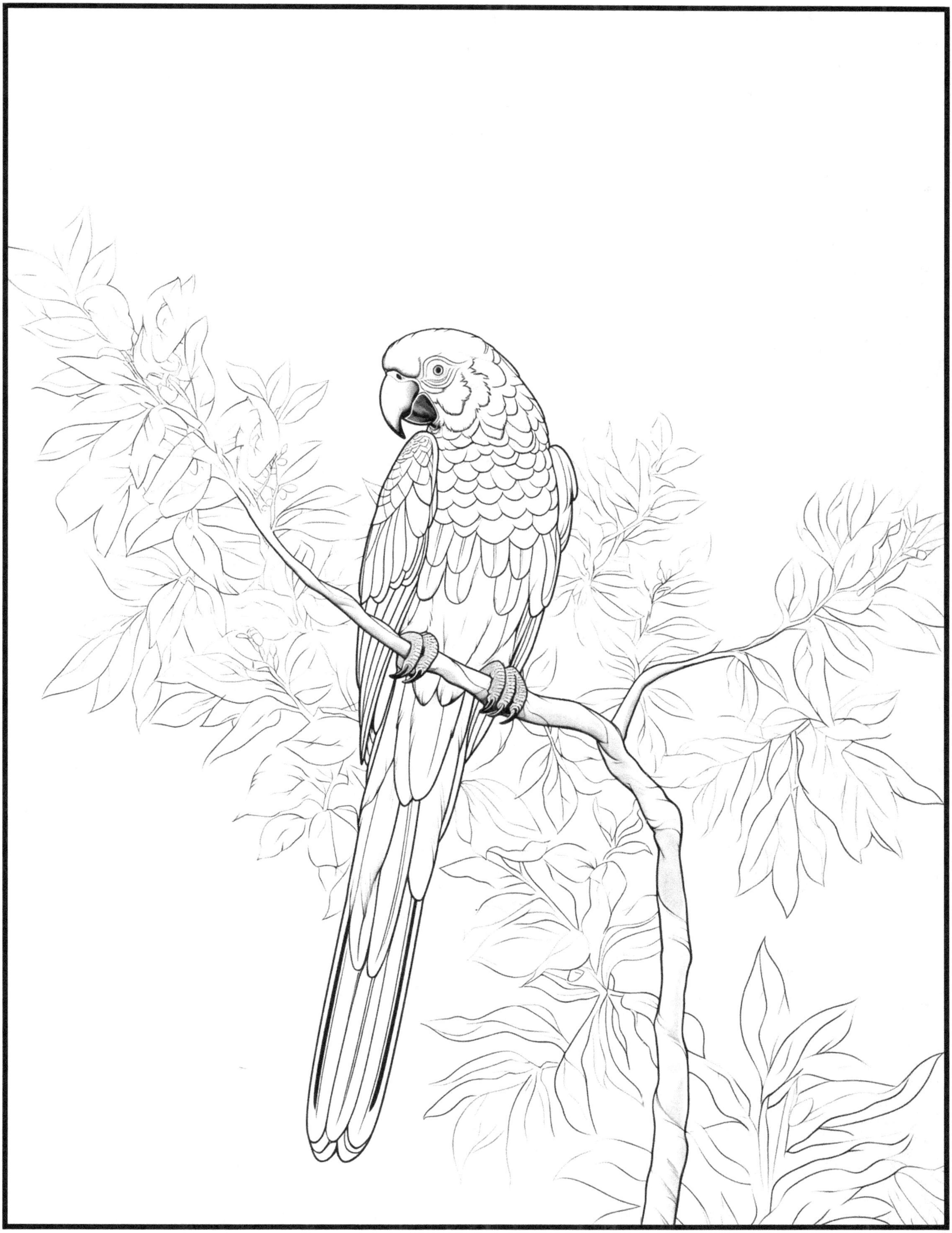

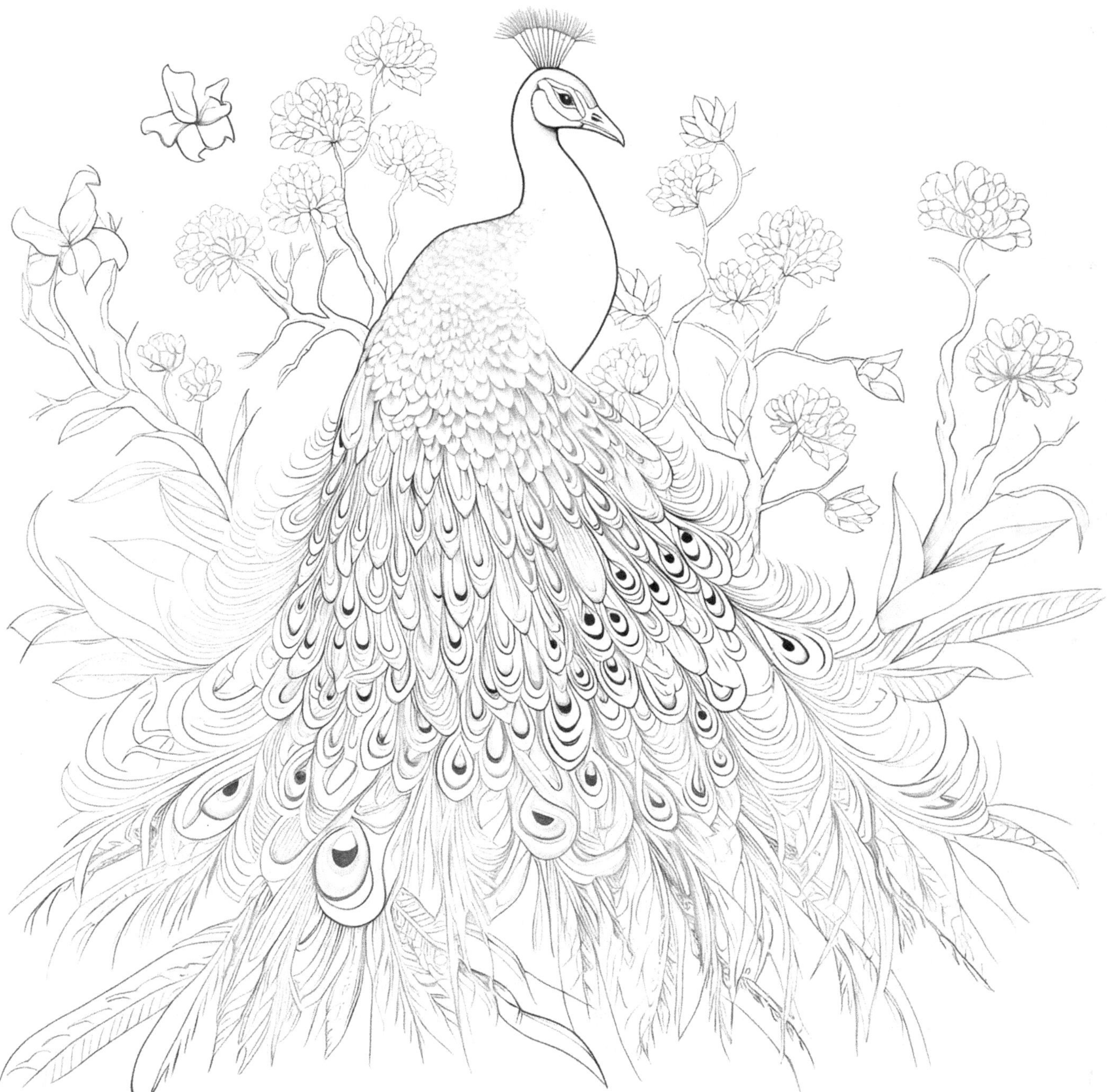

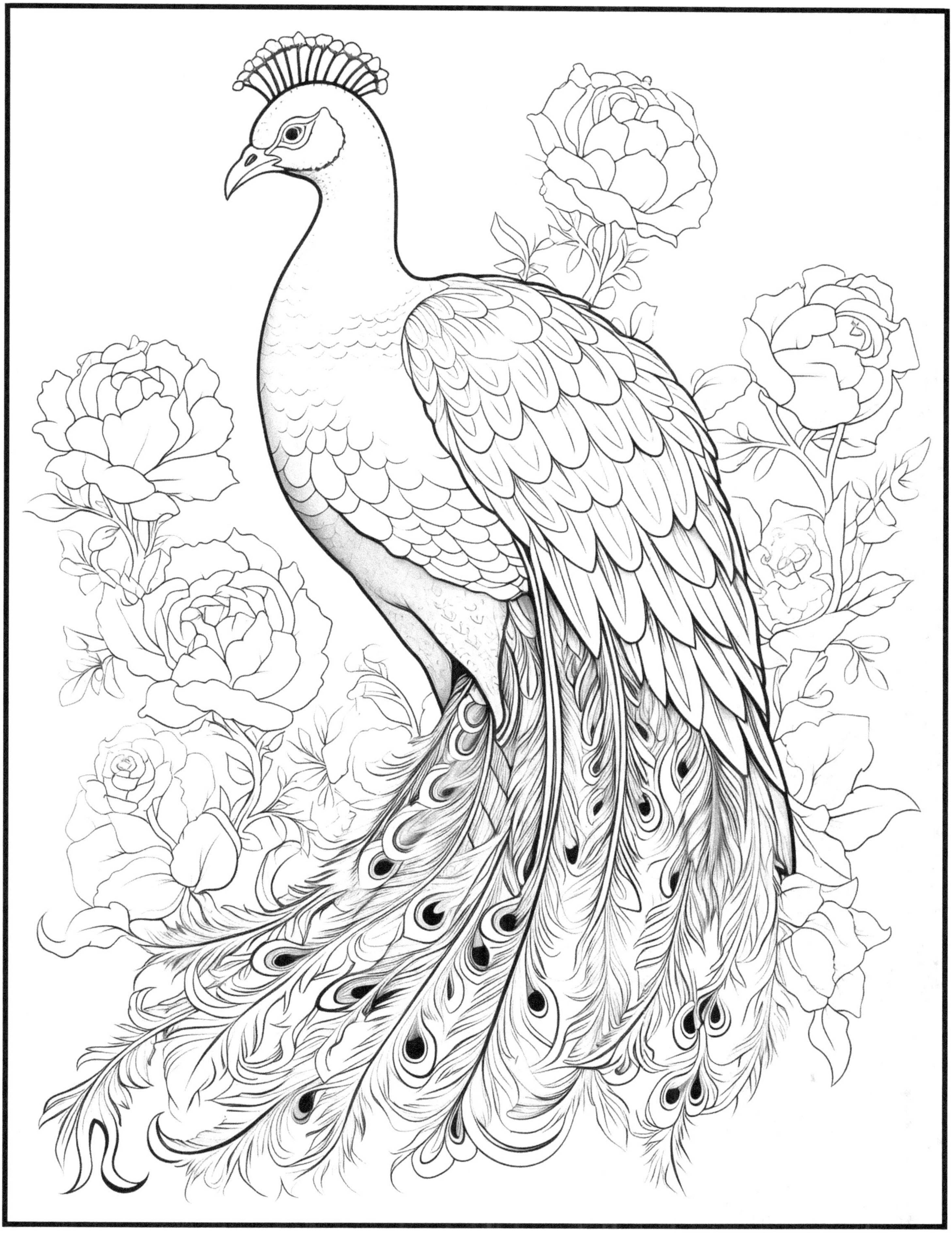

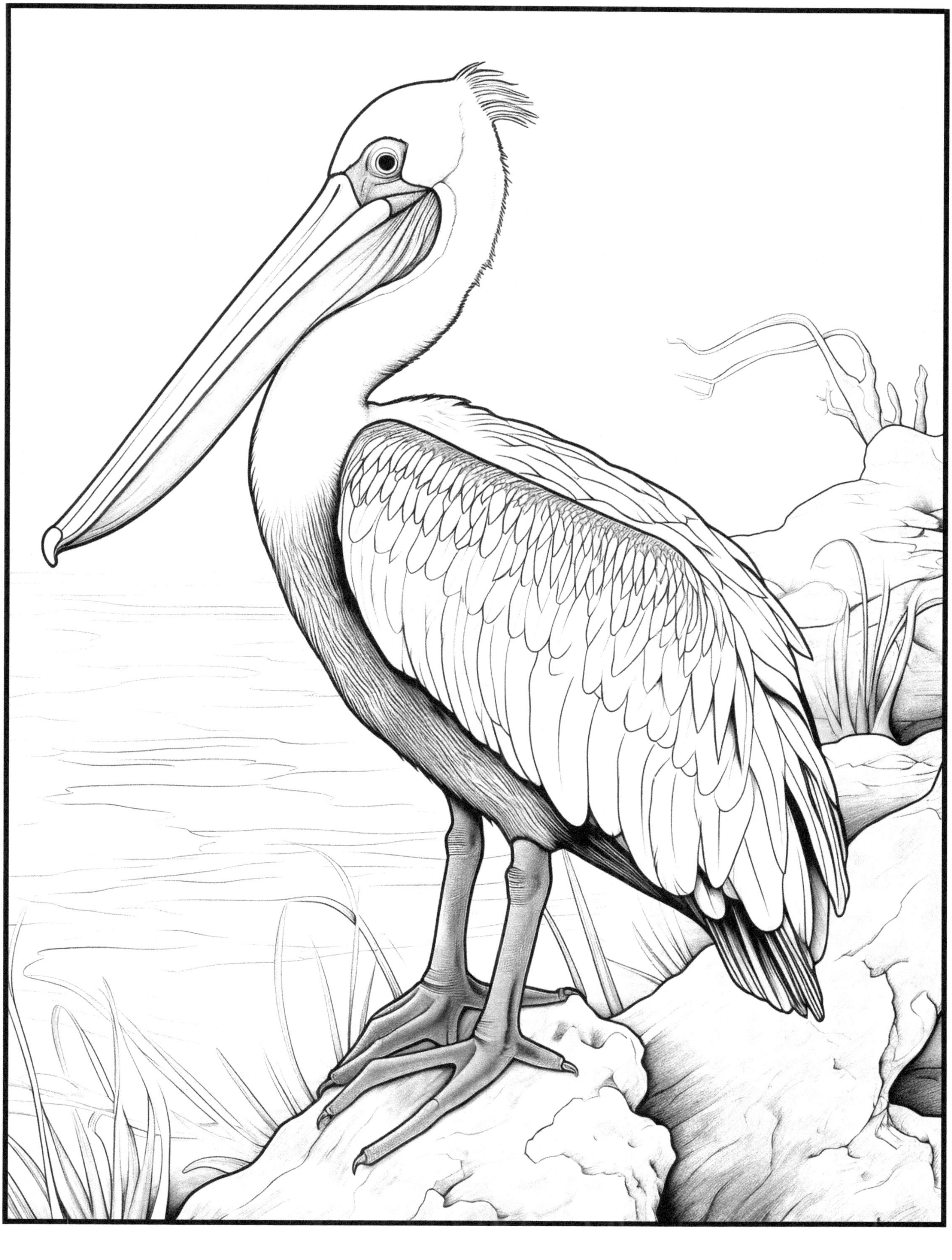

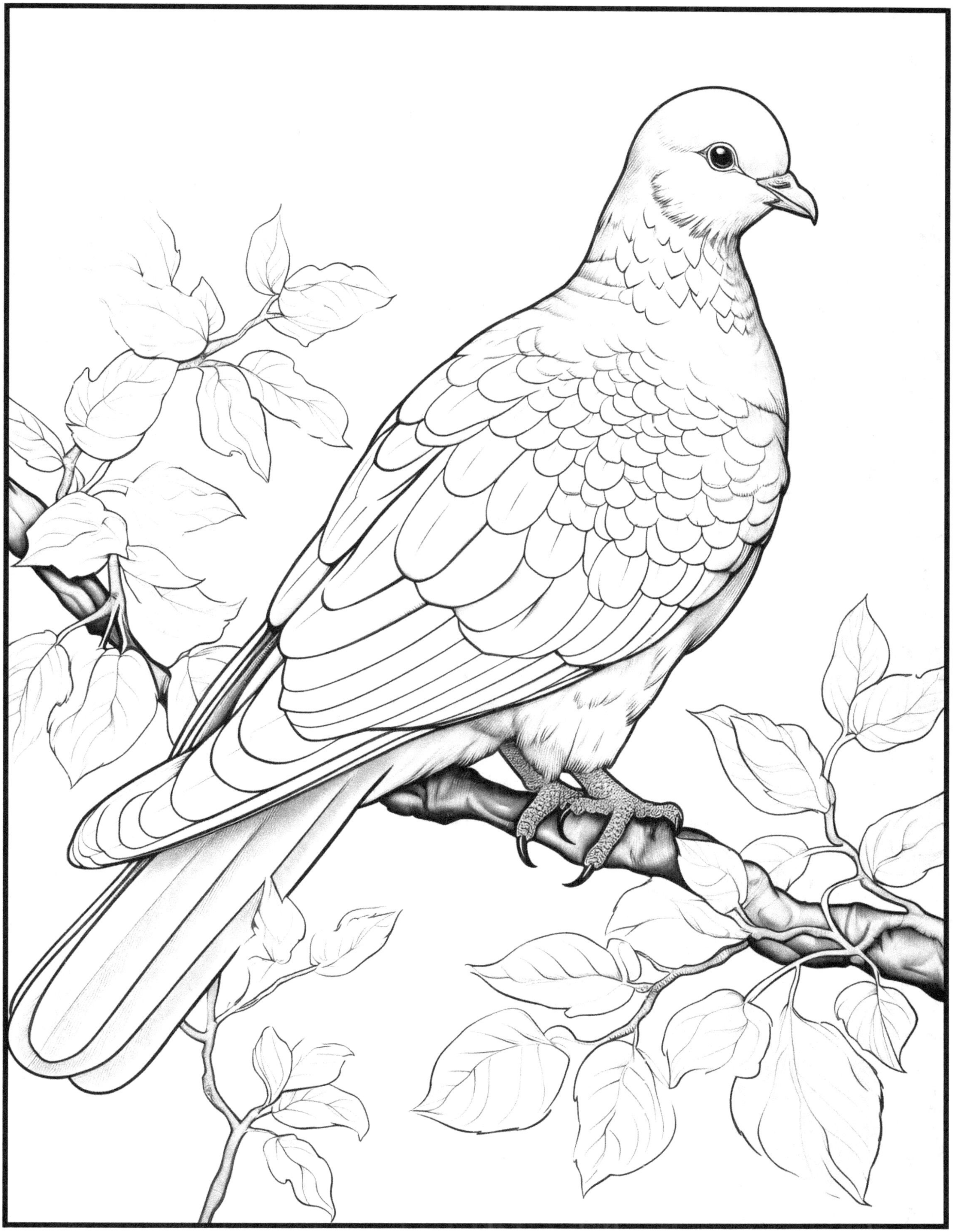

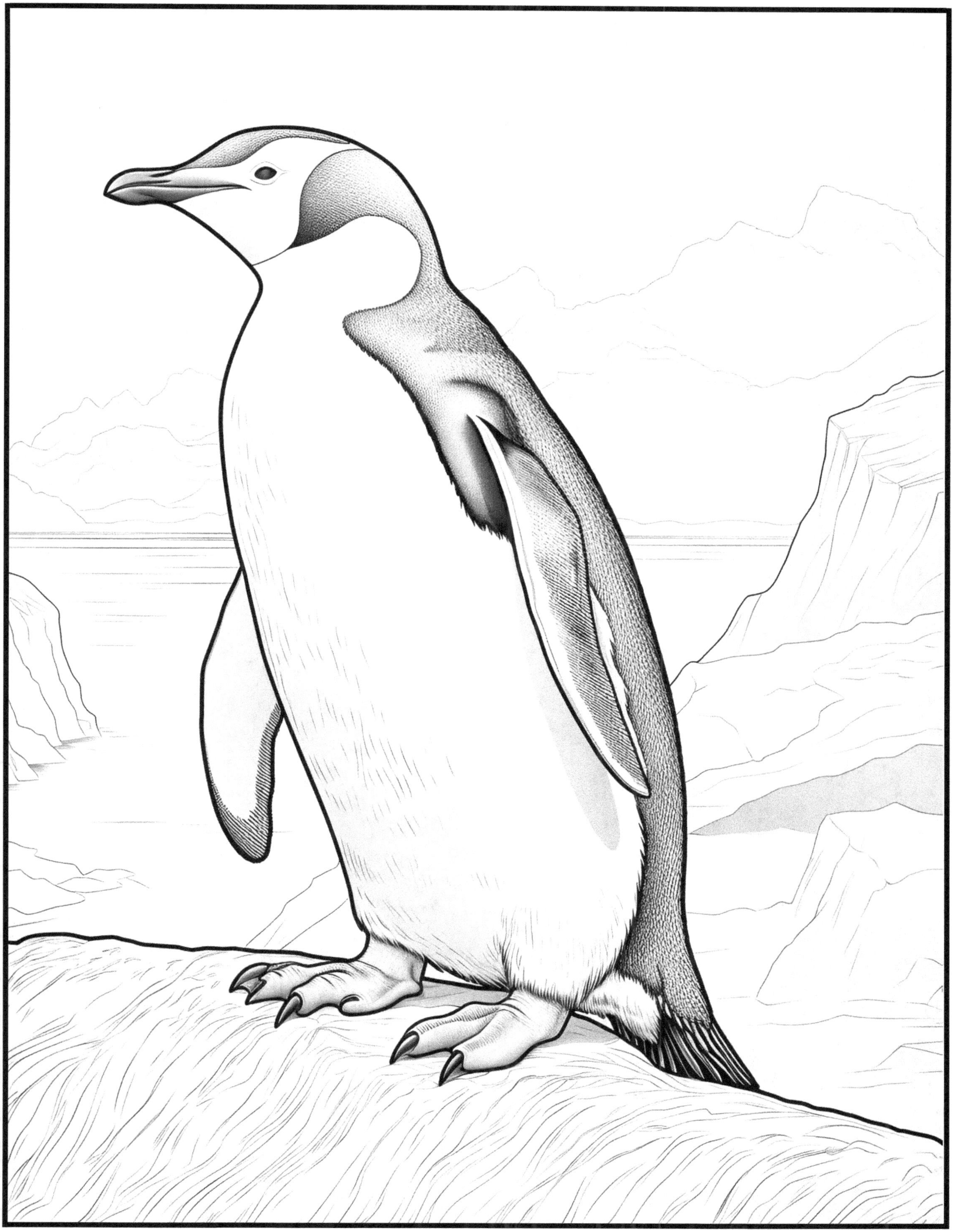

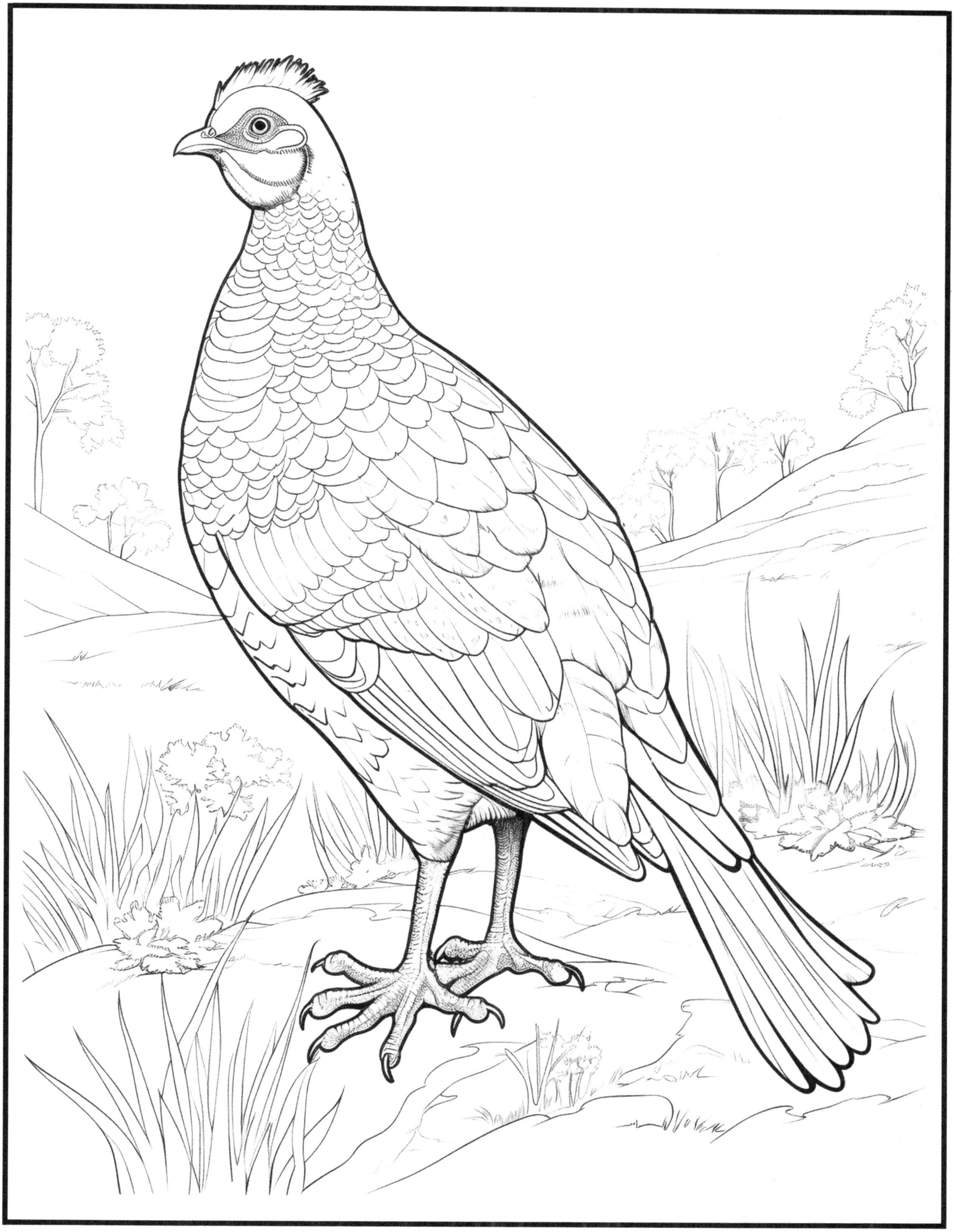

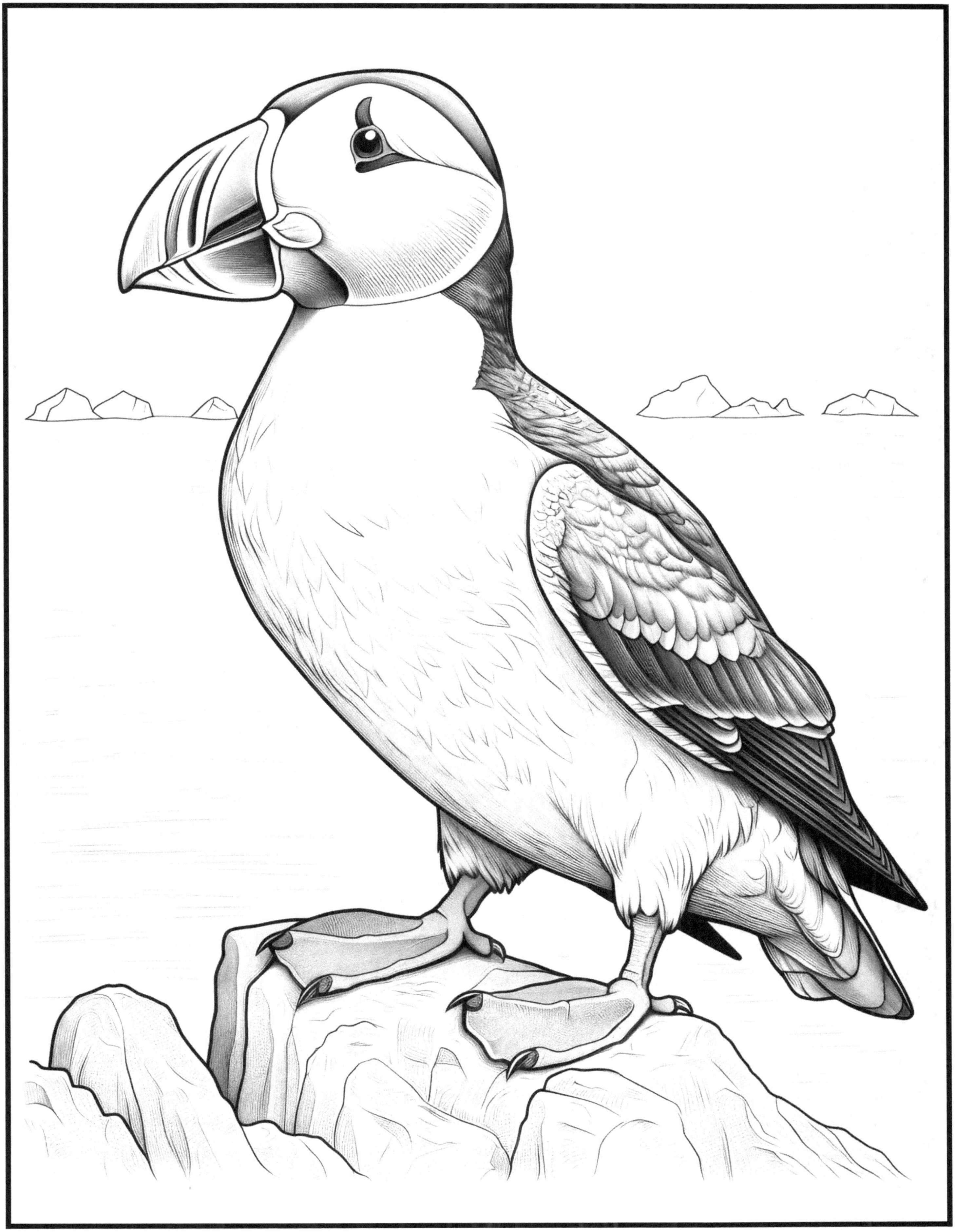

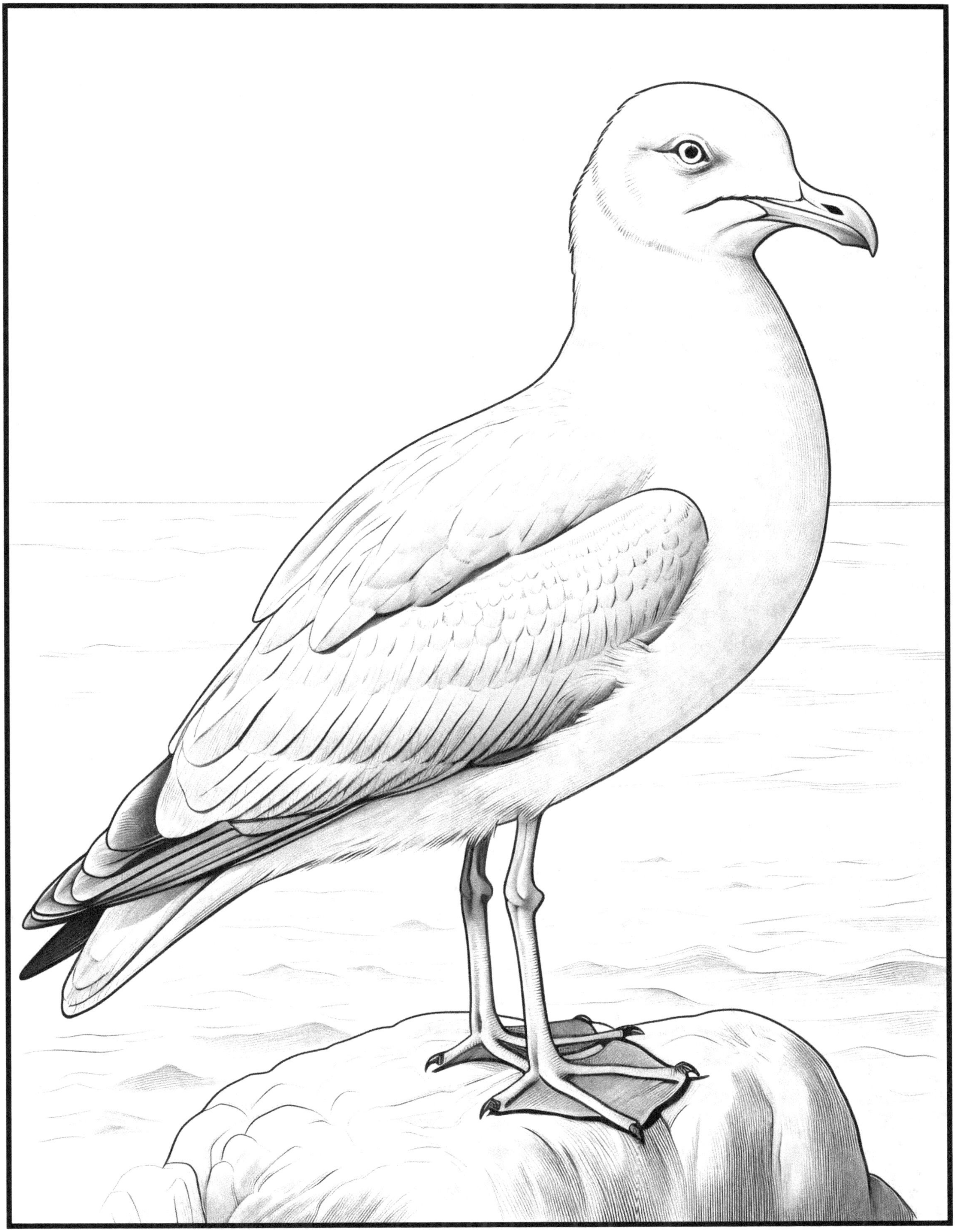

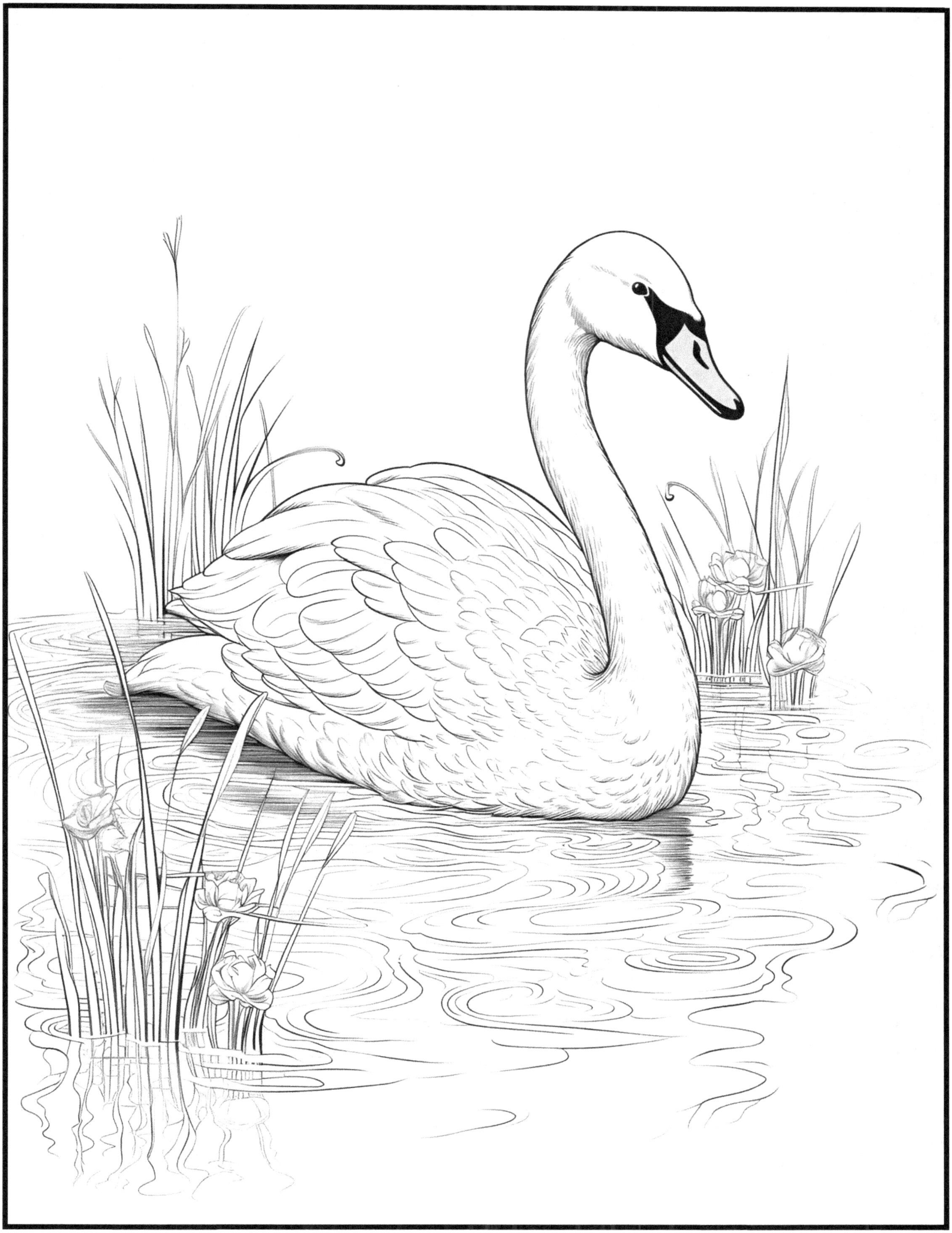

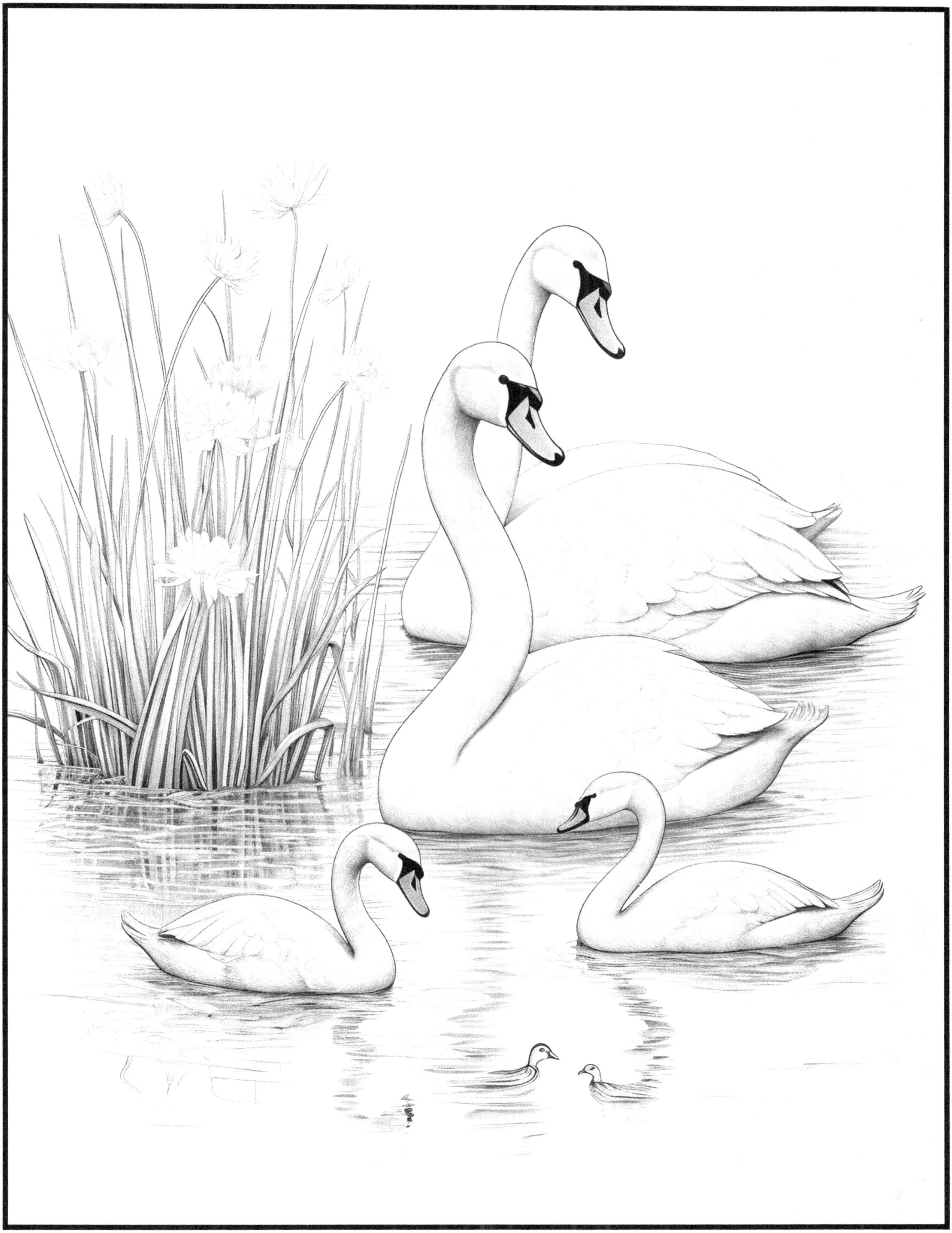

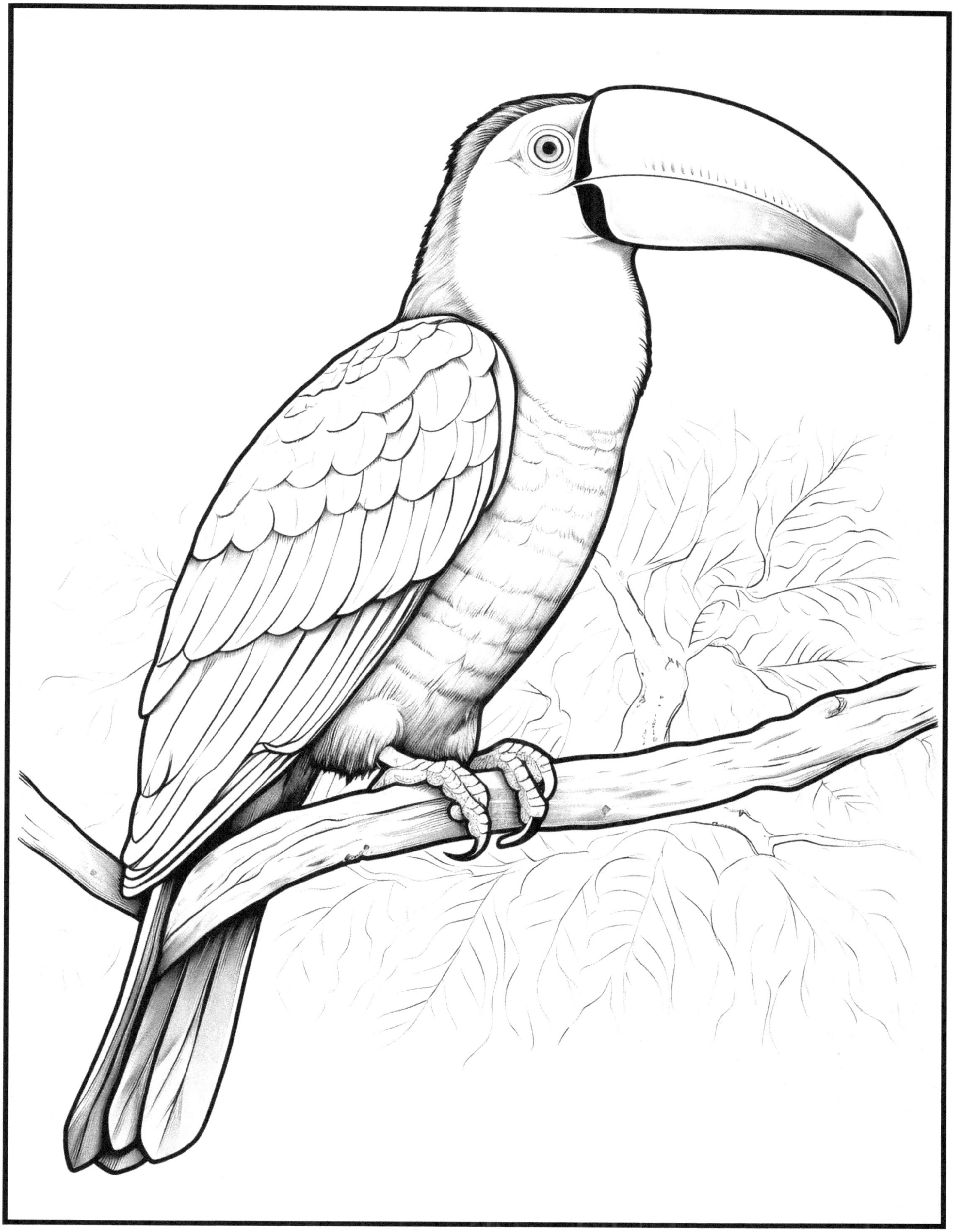

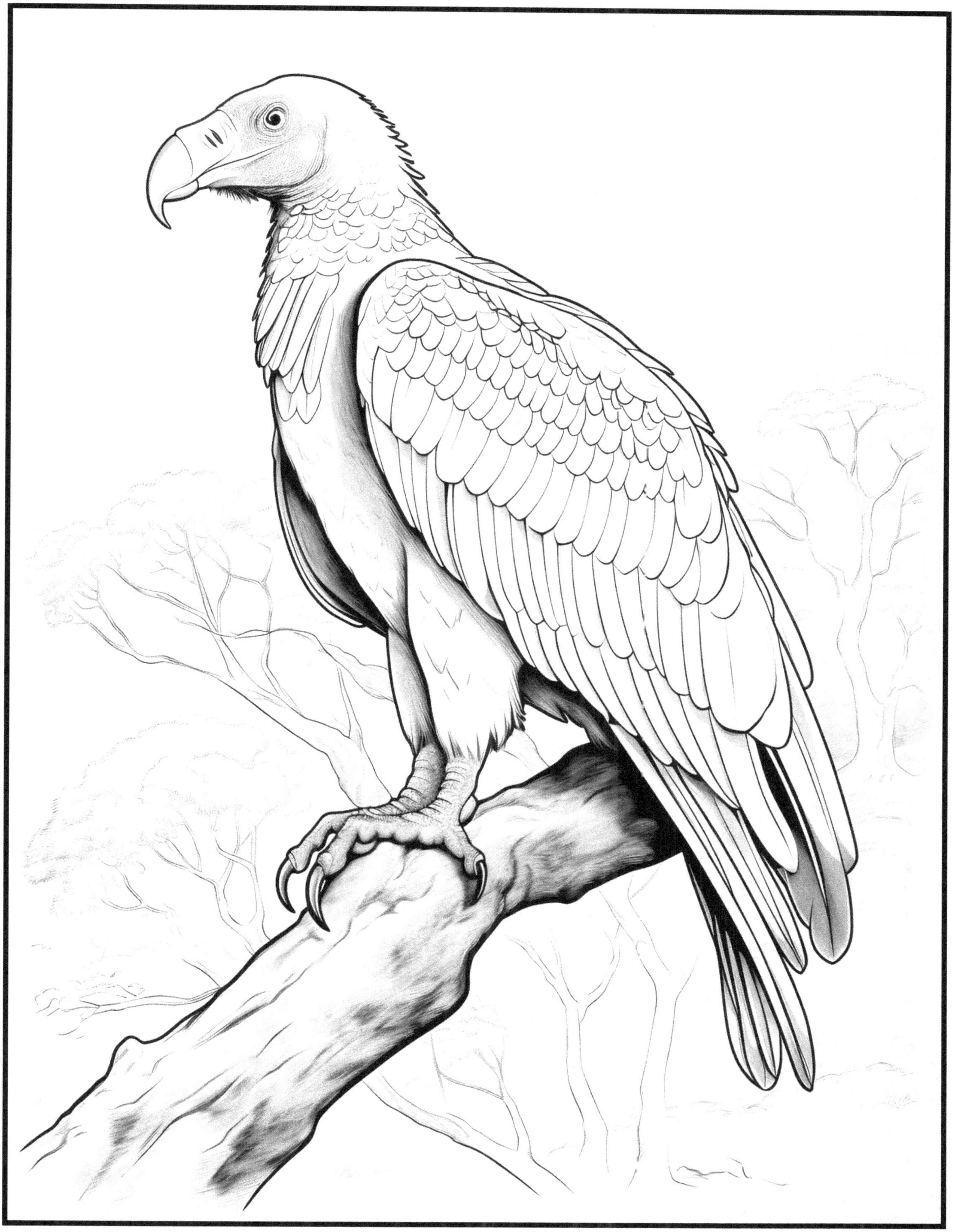

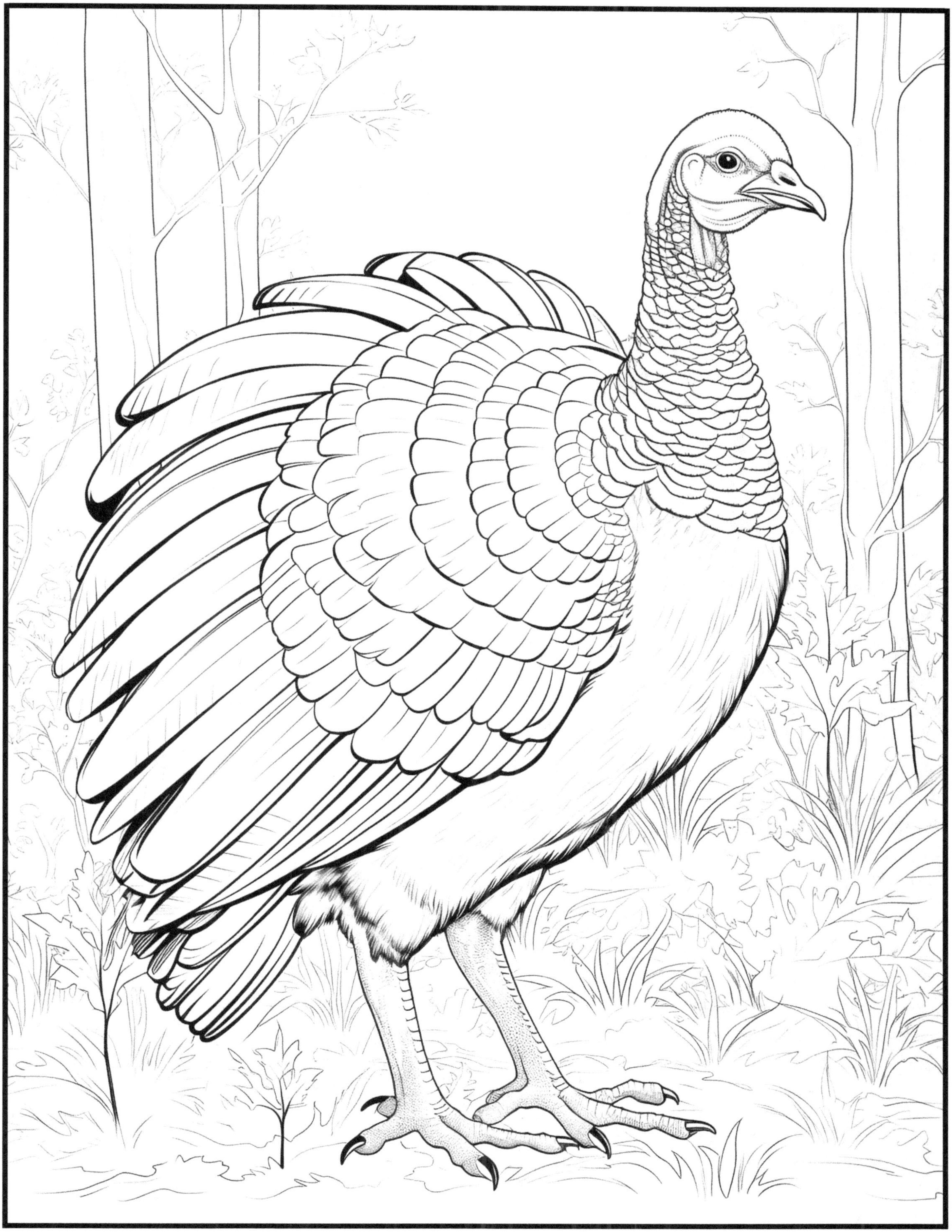

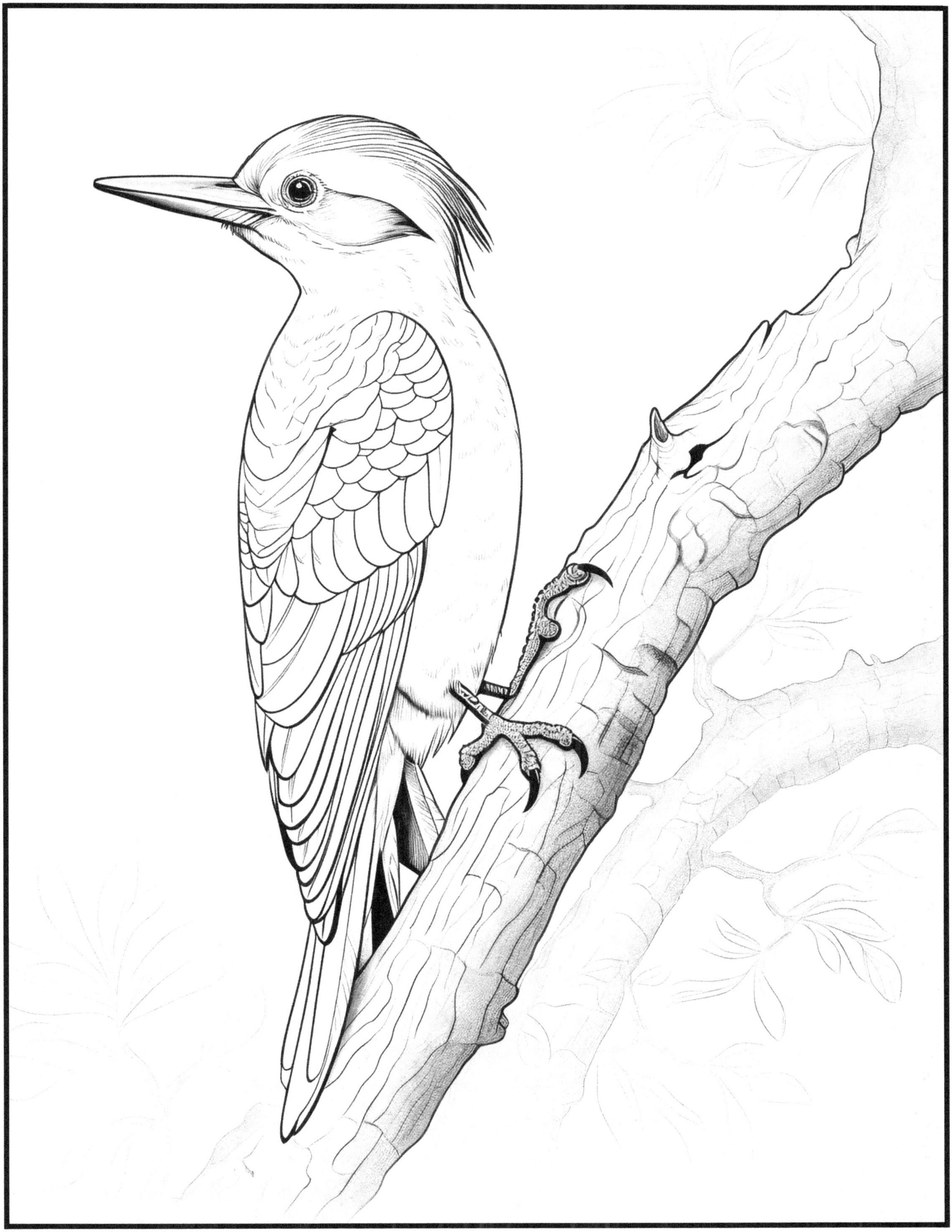

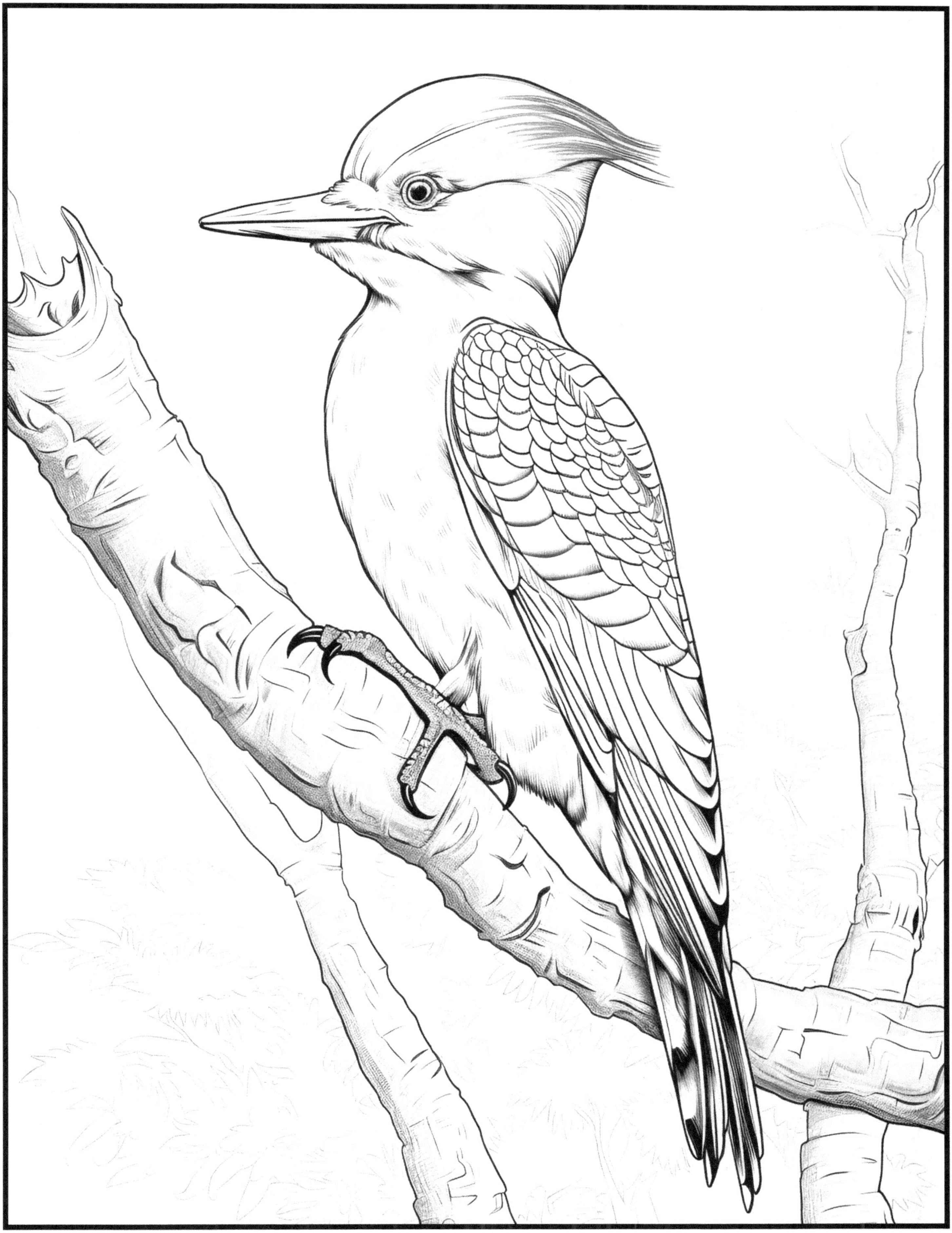

Dedicate to Bird Lover’s.

www.ingramcontent.com/pod-product-compliance
Lightning Source LLC
Chambersburg PA
CBHW080103010626
45794CB00014B/3073
9798857840511